NEW LIGHT FROM THE PROPHETS

NEW LIGHT FROM THE PROPHETS

by
LOUIS FINKELSTEIN

BASIC BOOKS, INC., PUBLISHERS
— NEW YORK

To my beloved colleagues,
the members of the Rabbinical Assembly,
for whose dedication, affection and scholarship I am
deeply grateful, and from whom
I learn so much.

CONTENTS

FOREWORD

The realization that portions of the Rabbinical tradition were actually composed by contemporaries of the Prophets or even the Prophets themselves may startle the reader of this work, as it startled me.

The thesis of this work has significant implications for the history of Jewish theology and literature, for the development of the Jewish system of education, and for an understanding of life in pre-Exilic and Exilic times. These implications will have to be explored and illumined, especially as new materal deriving from the Prophetic ages is recovered from its present matrix in the later literature.

The value of these studies for Hebrew philology will have to be appraised with particular care. In Chapter IX, I believe I have demonstrated that the word *mishmarot* is used in Mishna *Ta'anit* 4.2 in a sense it could have had only before the Babylonian Exile. The terms "Prophets" and "Early Prophets" were employed by the transmitters of the documents discussed in this volume, in passages where they can refer only to contemporaries. The principle that the precise words of early authorities should be preserved is articulated in the Mishnaic norm requiring a disciple to use the very diction of his master (Mishna *Eduyyot* 1.3). That the Rabbinic authorities usually obeyed this injunction has been shown by the late J. N. Epstein and Professor Louis Ginzberg as well as other scholars.

Nevertheless, particularly in aggadic passages, transmitters sometimes substituted contemporary terms for older ones. Thus in Chapter XI, I have shown how the term *qibbel* ("he received") describing the relation of a disciple to his master, though still preserved in ARN II throughout the discussion of the transmission of the tradition, was changed in Mishna *Abot* to indicate that the master "handed it down" to his disciple (*u-mesarah*).

Whether a particular word used in the documents discussed in this book belonged to the vocabulary of pre-Exilic Hebrew or not, will, therefore, have to be studied carefully. The mere occurence of a specific word in these texts cannot demonstrate its use in biblical times; nor can that fact disprove the antiquity of a text, in the light of other evidence.

I have deliberately limited the discussion in this volume to texts in which the Prophets are mentioned. Other texts appear to be of equal antiquity. But discussion of them must be postponed to another work, to permit full analysis of their origin, and their relation to the Prophets and the Pharisees.

Publication of this book has been delayed for some years, and might have been further delayed, except for the urging of some of my colleagues at the Seminary, particularly Professor Saul Lieberman. I do not, however, impute either to him or to anyone else any responsibility for the conclusions reached.

The volume was also read in manuscript by other friends, whose questions and suggestions were helpful. They include Professor Daniel Greenberg and Miss Jessica Feingold. Mrs. William Catlin read the proofs of the book, and Mr. Leslie Freedman prepared the Index.

The material was used as basis for a series of discussions at the Annual Convention of the Rabbinical Assembly at Kiamesha Lake, New York, in March 1969. Many Rabbis present raised important questions, with which I deal in the text.

This volume is part of the series published with the aid of the Stroock Publication Fund established at The Jewish Theological Seminary of America in memory of my beloved friend Sol. M. Stroock, by his children.

For the sake of consistency, I have generally cited biblical passages as they occur in "The Holy Scriptures", published by the Jewish Publication Society. The transliteration follows in general that used in *The Pharisees* and in *Akiba*. When reference is made in this volume to *The Pharisees* or *Akiba*, I, of course, have in mind my own works bearing these names.

In conclusion, let me once again pray, with the famous Sage, that "No error may be caused through me, that I may not be misled in any decision, and that my colleagues may find joy in my work."

Fourteenth day of Iyyar, 5729; the twenty-ninth day of the Omer. May 2, 1969

LOUIS FINKELSTEIN

CHAPTER I

INTRODUCTION

Walking through the streets of Jerusalem several years ago, pondering on the Prophets of Israel and their mighty achievements, I was suddenly privileged to glimpse a hitherto unrecognised facet of their labours. As if an ultraviolet light had brought illegible letters into view, numerous passages, long obscure, developed meaning because for the first time I realised they were actually composed before the Babylonian Exile rather than in the second or third century C.E. The purpose of this book is to offer proof for this unexpected insight, and to study some of its implications for future research.

Like the bricks and stones of ancient palaces, these words of the Prophets were incorporated into later structures where they have remained hidden for centuries. Some of the bricks are in fragments, some of the stones are chipped; but once their true origins are recognised, their significance is unmistakably clear.

To the magnificence of the poetry of the Prophets and the inspiration of their rhetoric, must now be added the greatness of their academic teaching which raised disciples who became teachers of succeeding generations of teachers.

The record of their accomplishment thus exceeded anything before conceived as possible. Their pre-eminence as moulders of the human mind and spirit remains unchallenged. But beyond that, we now discover in them precursors of the Sages of Israel, whose method of study and argument produced the great Rabbinic works, and fashioned the Jewish way of life.

What a singular combination of genius and inspiration was granted these astonishing people! After centuries—even in translation from the inspired original—the words of the Prophets can bring tears at one moment and offer healing comfort the next. Jeremiah, describing the unnecessary wars and sufferings of his day, moves from climax to climax until he breaks down: "Would that my head were water, and my eyes a very fountain of tears, that I might weep day and night, for the slain of the daughter of my people" (Jer. 8.23). Having repeated the words thousands of times since childhood, I am unfailingly stirred by their simple beauty, and their unique reflection of the agony to which all human life is exposed. Would that *my* head were water, and *my* eyes a very fountain of tears, that I might weep day and night for the slain of the daughter of *my* people and *my* generation.

But immediately after that reflection, comes recovery through the soothing cadences of Isaiah. "Comfort ye, comfort ye, My people, saith your God. Speak to the heart of Jerusalem and call to her; for she has completed her time of service; for her sin has been forgiven. For she has received from the Lord's hands double her sins" (Isa. 1). The healing is aided by chanting the ancient verses in the traditional soothing hum of a mother lulling a child to sleep: *"nahamu, nahamu ammi, yomar elohekem. . . ."*

How privileged were the artisans and traders of the Jerusalem market place and the peasants of Judah and Ephraim to be the first targets of an oratory that rings down the centuries, across the oceans and continents of the world! And how little did those ancients realise that through them the Prophets—whom they both loved and disdained—were channelling a divine message to peoples yet unborn!

As rhetoricians and poets, the Prophets of Israel are unsurpassed in either sacred or profane literature; and the content of their message is as eternal as their music is penetrating and inspiring. The revolution they inaugurated in human thought was one of the very few which really changed men's lives, ultimately creating a new world out of the ashes of the old. The process has been slow, and only now, after millenia, are we approaching the Age of the Common Man, who has been utterly disregarded throughout history. Only now are we beginning to accept in our minds and in our hearts the doctrine of the Prophet Amos: "Are ye not like the children of the Ethiopians unto Me, O children of Israel?" (Amos 9.7). We are fumbling to translate into institutions

2

and attitudes the words in which Isaiah sums up his whole philosophy of human relations: "Blessed be Egypt My people, and Assyria the work of My hands, and Israel Mine inheritance" (Isa. 25).

Yet, as the present volume will show, all we have known about these supreme geniuses was peripheral to their fundamental task, that of teaching in their academies, raising disciples, and transforming them into teachers of other disciples. Behind the great addresses and poems preserved in the Scriptures, and differing from the generalised ethical appeals to the public, there was oral instruction, intended to create an unshakeable inner nucleus of devotion to truth, to learning, and to human betterment, as complete as might realistically be attainable among men.

The documents discussed in this volume are probably only a few of those awaiting extrication from concealment in later traditions. Yet this sampling reveals a forgotten splendour of learning and insight, of greatness beyond any greatness imaginable. The Prophets emerge as institution-builders, teachers, religious statesmen, authors of prayers on the one hand and learned tracts on the other. Beyond denouncing the evil in their time they were founders of a better society. The Messianic Age, which they predicted and for which they longed, was expected to burst upon the world after slow and prolonged preparations, through gradual but realistic emancipation of their followers from the enticements of the common corruption.

It is the thesis of this study that in addition to their public labours, which were known to the whole community, the Prophets conducted academies for their immediate disciples, where teachings were not written but were studied by rote. The memorised texts entered the heritage of the Prophetic schools. Handed down from master to disciple for centuries, they were integrated ultimately into what became Pharisaic and Rabbinic works, and—perhaps thirteen centuries after their composition—were put into writing. With some labour, part of the original compositions (as will be shown), may be isolated from later accretions, themselves valuable and instructive.

The student approaching this work will doubtless share

3

my own original scepticism regarding the thesis which gradually unfolded itself to me. Only with great difficulty could I free myself from the preconceptions regarding the origin of the Rabbinic works under consideration. It was hard to believe that views sanctioned by great scholars, and which had persisted since my youth, had to be modified, deepened, and broadened.[1]

The reader of the present volume may rightly pose significant questions: Is it possible that so much greatness was disproportionately and extravagantly granted to so few —poured out in a poor, tiny land on the rim of the desert? Have their words preserved in writing revealed but one facet of the Prophets' instruction? Were they more than inspired poets with uncanny insight into the future, more than imaginative statesmen able to foresee much that was hidden from professional diplomats? Is the example of the Prophets, who were so imbued with love for mankind and faith in the right that they courted martyrdom as the only hope for salvation, still valid for a troubled generation living in a totally different world thousands of years later? Could men on whom so many gifts of mind and spirit were divinely lavished possess yet another dimension unsuspected before our day? Supreme theologians, moralists, historians, and philosophers of history; fearless opponents of tyranny and injustice; lovers of peace in a world of war, and of justice in a world of violence, could the Prophets add still another to the list of their vital services to man and God?

Talmudic authorities frequently described the Prophets as teachers and heads of academies. But this imagery has always been considered a projection of contemporary life on to the past. That Isaiah walked to and fro in his Academy when the divine voice came to him had seemed a delightful poetic vision, an unforgettable description, instructive only regarding the thought and mind of the narrator and without relevance to facts.

However, the documents cited will show that the Prophets actually led double lives. To the general community they appeared in the guise of their writings, meant to influence public opinion, to guide the affairs of state, to change the private and public behaviour of leaders and masses. To achieve these purposes, the Prophets employed superb imagination and poetry. They sang their messages. Ezekiel (33.32) tells us that many came for entertainment, to listen as at a concert, not to be instructed but simply to be lifted out of self for a moment. To have influence in his own time, the Prophet had to enunciate ideals attainable only in a Messianic Age, unrelated to the practical realities of a mundane, secular world; he had to paint in the most enticing colours the ultimate glories which awaited man in order to stir him to effort.

But in the privacy of their schools, surrounded by intimate disciples, these imaginative orators became teachers of specific norms. The glittering generalities of the public forum were replaced by realistic discussions of immediate personal issues and the formulation of goals realisable for great men. How should one pray, and how should one prepare oneself for prayer? What authority was to be allowed Temple priests in the regulation of the religious and moral tenets of the people? In what order should the priestly class minister at the Temple? What was the responsibility of the individual Israelite in the Temple worship? Were pagans capable of prophecy? Could a gentile be king over Israel? Could a woman be monarch in her own right? Is study the obligation of all, rich and poor alike? Or is it only for privileged groups, the poor being left to concentrate on responsibility for their families? Precisely as in the later Pharisaic and Rabbinic schools, answers were sought in the interpretation of Scriptural verses. Implications of the passages from the Pentateuch were discussed. Whenever possible, norms were formulated to reduce the complications of moral and ritualistic judgments to the utmost simplicity, to precise formulas easy to recall.

That so vast an area of the Prophets' activity should for so long have remained hidden from scholars and historians will, at first glance, seem almost as incredible as the historical fact of the activity itself. But a study of the documents discussed here will show that the incredible actually happened. When considered as emanating from Rabbinic times, or from those immediately preceding the Talmudic Sages, each passage presented difficult problems to later students. Some could not be precisely reconciled with the rest of the Talmudic tradition. Some spoke of the Prophets and the immediate disciples of the Prophets as contemporaries. Some alluded to institutions unknown to the Talmudic tradition. At least one was explicitly described as pre-Exilic in a norm which was itself composed no later than the fifth or fourth century B.C.E. In each instance, the difficulty had been smoothed over through centuries of transmission and commentary. Reading the printed texts of the Mishna, *Tosefta, Sifre,* or *Mekilta,* especially with their commentators, one was often completely unaware of the real difficulties in the text, just as a reader of a translation is unaware of the sufferings of the student struggling with the original.

The twentieth century has supplied the researcher with many new tools for the recovery of these hidden documents. Some derive from increasing knowledge based on the results of recent archaeology. Others belong to the realm of psychology, and particularly to rural and urban sociology. Still others, perhaps the most important of all, relate to the scientific study of ancient texts. The premise of this study must always be respect for the original author of a text, as well as for the transmitter and the copyist.

Wanton emendations of the *textus receptus* and loose accusations of erroneous readings frequently lead to further obfuscation of the original. But careful study of the habitual ways of each copyist, his characteristic omissions and insertions as well as his overall style and, above all, comparison of different texts and sources, will sometimes make possible the recovery of the *ipsissima verba* of the original authors and of the ancient oral tradition. In the study of the documents involved in the present research, particular help came from Solomon Schechter's exploration of the Cairo *Genizah,* through which thousands of manuscripts were brought to Cambridge University. No less significant were the tireless efforts of the late Professor Louis Ginzberg and Professor J. N. Epstein (of Jerusalem) who utilized this hoard of manuscripts as well as other manuscript material for the recovery of original readings of the ancient texts, particularly of the Mishna, and in certain measure also of the *Yerushalmi.*

Among living scholars Professor Saul Lieberman should be especially singled out, for (as shown in the notes) his work is indispensable to the present book, as it is to any effective research in ancient Rabbinic literature. He has not only sharpened methods for critical study of Rabbinic texts and elucidated numerous obscurities, but has courageously illumined many passages which exegetical ingenuity has left—in the terminology of contemporary schools—*satum* ("sealed").

For a number of years I have been engaged in the preparation of scientific editions of the *Sifre* and *Sifra*. All the manuscript material required for the preparation of these works was brought together through the generosity of various librarians and the American Council of Learned Societies, to which I cannot sufficiently express my gratitude. While still quite young I was able to find all the manuscript material, scattered in so many libraries, largely through the help of Professor Alexander Marx who had painstakingly read innumerable catalogues, and kept their contents stored in his prodigious memory.

Generally the manuscript material helped illumine the text by providing better readings than were found in the printed edition. But it had always struck me as curious that sometimes the establishment of the early texts only made matters more difficult. Although I have been engaged in the study of these works since 1923, it was only, as already remarked, many years later that I realised that such passages as the one discussed in Chapter II, which made no sense if ascribed to an author of the second or third century C.E., became intelligible if one postulated a pre-Exilic author.

After some inner struggle, I allowed the clue to lead me on, and again read through all the Tannaitic *Midrashim* as well as the *Abot of R. Nathan* with one question uppermost in my mind: Was the document just mentioned unique in its apparently pre-Exilic origin, or were there others like it? Finally, I decided to re-study Professor Saul Lieberman's edition of *Tosefta Zeraim* and *Moed,* with his great commentary, *Tosefta Kifeshutah,* having the same question in mind. Some of the results of this investigation, which occupied several years, are summarised in the present work. Not all the documents which, in my opinion, bear the stamp of pre-Exilic, Prophetic authorship are presented here. The others, also probably pre-Exilic, require further investigation to establish the full significance of their original readings. However, it does not seem right to withhold publication of the present study because of the difficulties involved in fully understanding other texts.

The present study will demonstrate that some of the material examined dates from the fifth and fourth centuries B.C.E.; some from the period of the Babylonian Exile (586-538 B.C.E.); and some from pre-Exilic times, as early as the reign of King Josiah (638-607 B.C.E.) or even the reigns of Kings Manasseh (691-640 B.C.E.) and Amon (640-638 B.C.E.).

All the documents bear the stamp of Prophetic authorship, and were transmitted orally in the Prophetic schools. Some are commentaries on portions of the Pentateuch; one is a passage from Mishna *Abot;* another is from Mishna *Ta'anit.* The discovery of these ancient, Prophetic works in the midst of the later Rabbinic literature should, on consideration, not surprise scholars of this generation. The Dead Sea Scrolls have shown that the midrashic method was common in some Judean circles as early as the second century B.C.E.[2] My analysis of the Passover *Haggadah* has demonstrated that similar *Midrashim* were composed even earlier, in the age of the Ptolemy.[3] A glance at the Book of Jubilees[4] shows that its author made use of very early *Midrashim,* otherwise known only from works of the third century C.E. onward.[5] It has long been known that the authors of the Septuagint utilised midrashic interpretations of various verses in the Pentateuch.[6] The Book of Chronicles frequently indulges in midrashic interpretations of the Pentateuch.[7] As J. N. Epstein[8] has shown, when Haggai asked the priests "Torah" (Hag. 2.11), he was raising a question not about the written Pentateuchal legislation, but about its interpretation in a *Midrash.*

Other evidence shows that some passages in the Mishna, *Tosefta,* and Tannaitic *Midrashim* derive from very early periods such as the fifth or fourth century B.C.E. Thus it can be demonstrated that some norms in *Tosefta* were composed when the Tetragrammaton was still pronounced in its original form in the Synagogue and possibly in home services.

8

This would mean that their authors flourished before the time of the Chronicler, who regularly employs a cypher for the Tetragrammaton;[9] probably before the compilation of the last four books of the Psalms, where such a cypher is likewise used;[10] and before the time of the Septuagint, which regularly renders the Tetragrammaton by "the Lord," a translation of the cypher currently in use in the Synagogue.

One of these passages is found in *Tosefta Berakot* 6 (7) 20 (ed. Lieberman p. 39). It reads : "One who begins a prayer with *yod heh* [i.e. the Tetragrammaton, actually enunciating it] and ends with *yod heh* [in the doxology] is a Sage.[11] [One who begins] with *yod heh* and ends with *'aleph lamed* [the cypher *'elohim*] is ignorant.[12] [One who begins] with *'aleph lamed* and ends with *yod heh* is an average person.[13] One who begins with *'aleph lamed* and ends with *'aleph lamed* is following another way [i.e., is a sectarian]."[14] This *baraita* also occurs in *Yer. Berakot* 9.1, 1d, with some textual variants.

Clearly the *baraita* was composed when prayers in the Synagogue contained the Tetragrammaton in the opening phrase and in the doxology, for surely the authors considered the prescribed prayers those of "a Sage." The composers of this *baraita* evidently knew also of a widespread custom to substitute the cypher *'aleph lamed* for the Tetragrammaton in the beginning of the Synagogue prayer, but they had apparently never heard of the use of the cypher *'aleph dalet*, now current.

The custom denounced as sectarian was actually followed, as Professor Saul Lieberman has shown,[15] by the sect of the Dead Sea Scrolls. However, it was probably not invented by them, for the *baraita* presumably antedates their origin by generations, perhaps by centuries. They simply adopted a custom followed by some groups, but which the authors of the *baraita* disapproved and called heretical.

It is likewise evident that the final passage cited in *Tosefta Yadaim* (2.20, ed. Zuckermandel p. 684) derives from the times when the Tetragrammaton was pronounced in the Synagogue. According to Ms. Vienna and the citation of Rabbi Samson of Sens, *Tosefta* reads :[16] "The Morning-Bathers say, 'We complain of you, O Pharisees, because you pronounce the Name before you bathe.' The Pharisees reply,

'We complain of you, O Morning-Bathers, because you mention the Name with a body which contains defilement.' "

There could be no complaint against the Pharisees or the Morning-Bathers if they did not actually pronounce the Name. The argument between the Pharisees and the Morning-Bathers apparently occurred, then, while both groups still pronounced the Tetragrammaton in prayer.

Several passages in *Mekilta* can immediately be seen to be of the same antiquity as that quoted from the Mishna. They deal with the *ger* whom they identify, as Scripture generally seems to do, with the landless stranger, often compelled to attach himself to a farmer, becoming virtually a serf.

Thus we read, with some astonishment, in *Mekilta Mishpatim,* Chapter 20 (p. 311), a comment on the following verse: "And ye shall be holy unto Me; therefore ye shall not eat any flesh that is torn of the beast in the field; ye shall cast it to the dogs" (Exod. 22.30). *Mekilta* says: "This is intended to teach you that the dog is honoured above the slave; for an animal torn by a beast is given to the dog, but the carcass of a dead animal is given to the slave."

The only passage from which one might infer that the carcass of a dead animal is to be fed to a slave is Deuteronomy 14.21, "Ye shall not eat anything that dieth of itself; thou mayest give it to the *ger* that is within thy gates, that he may eat it; or thou mayest sell it to a foreigner."

Mekilta thus interprets the word *ger* in the Deuteronomic verse to mean "slave." But the word cannot mean "slave" in the ordinary sense. Apparently at the time of the composition of this comment the landless *ger* held the position of a slave; he had to covenant himself as a serf to a landed farmer.

While the Talmud knows of a *ger toshab,* i.e., a proselyte who, having abandoned idol-worship, still did not bind himself to observe the commandments and was therefore not the equivalent of an Israelite, it normally interprets the word *ger* in Scripture to mean "proselyte." *Ger* could not have that meaning in the passage from Deuteronomy, where it must mean *ger toshab.* But it is surprising to find it interpreted to mean "slave," and even more amazing to read in a

Rabbinic text that a dog is superior to a slave!

The comment derives from circles far removed in outlook from the Pharisees and from the Rabbinic authorities. But the interpretation of the word *ger* in its biblical sense of landless stranger also occurs in another passage of the same section of *Mekilta* (p. 311). The verse under discussion in that passage is Exodus 22.20, "And a *ger* thou shalt not wrong, neither shalt thou oppress him; for ye were *gerim* in the land of Egypt." *Mekilta* says: "Thou shalt not oppress him with words, and shalt not wrong him in money matters. Therefore thou must not say to him, 'Yesterday thou wast worshipping *Bel*,[17] and pigs are squealing[18] from between thy teeth, and thou dost dare to argue with me.'" The notion that pigs "are squealing" between the teeth of the *ger* indicates that, although he no longer worshipped *Bel*, he still ate forbidden food. This fact must not be used in an argument as a taunt.

The passage thus derives from a time when a *ger* was not a proselyte, but a stranger who had given up the worship of idols. Because *ger* in later times came to mean "proselyte," the Mishna, citing this passage of *Mekilta*, paraphrases it. Therefore, the Mishna (*Baba Mezia* 4.10) says: "Just as there is deceit in money matters, so there is oppression in words. . . Thus one may not say to a repentant sinner, 'Remember your former deeds.' If one is a descendant of proselytes, one may not say to him, 'Remember the deeds of your ancestors,' for it is said, 'And a *ger* thou shalt not wrong, neither shalt thou oppress him.'"

The quotation of the verse as well as the content of the exhortation point to the *Mekilta* as the source of the Mishnaic norm. But the compiler of the Mishna had to change the text of *Mekilta*; for in his time, *ger* had come to mean proselyte. The change in the norm made in the Mishna was also adopted by the editors of *Sifra* (*Behar perek* 4.2, ed. Weiss 107d).

In the light of the interpretation of *ger* as the equivalent of serf, one can understand the interpretation of Deuteronomy 1.16 in *Sifre ad loc.* (*Sifre*, Deut. 16, p. 27). Scripture states that Moses commanded the judges whom he had appointed to "hear the causes between your brethren, and judge righteously, between a man and his brother, and his *ger*."

The expression "his *ger*" as though the *ger* could belong to someone, was disturbing. Therefore, *Sifre* suggests that the word might in this instance mean "his neighbour" or "his wedding attendant." But it also offers the explanation "his client" (*totab,* the Aramaic equivalent of *toshab*).

These uses of the word *ger,* in its earliest sense of the landless stranger whose status was that of a slave, cannot be reconciled with the institutions known to post-biblical Judaism, according to which a *ger* was a proselyte, with all the rights and privileges of any other Israelite. The passages in *Mekilta* thus date at the very latest from the fourth or fifth centuries B.C.E. With this evidence of very early norms and midrashic interpretations, it is not unnatural to discover midrashic and normative texts formulated even before the time of Haggai, and indeed by Prophets before the Exile.

The arguments will necessarily involve detailed analyses of the texts in question, and a reconstruction of their earliest readings from manuscripts and through the use of parallel sources. It will appear that only our preconceptions and the unavailability of manuscript readings and critical texts have mistakenly led us to treat them as products of the second and third centuries C.E.

The importance of the discovery of the Prophetic origin of these texts need hardly be urged. The analysis offered in this work demonstrates that the method of study in the Pharisaic schools was actually developed centuries before they became a recognised group. My contention that Pharisaism is Prophecy in action is now further corroborated through textual evidence which seems incontrovertible. But beyond this (as already observed), the Prophets emerge from this study as scholars, exegetes, teachers, and institution-builders. The quarrel of the Pharisaic scholars with the priests of Jerusalem was simply a sequel to that of the Prophets with the Temple priests of their time. The opposition of Prophet and priest involved more than being pro-Egyptian or pro-Babylonian. It involved the basic question of the authority to interpret the Mosaic law, and whether the Torah had been handed over to the priests or entrusted to Prophet-scholars.[19]

In one of the norms embedded in Mishna and *Tosefta,*

there seems to be a suggestion that the "Prophets of Jerusalem" formed a school by themselves, distinct from their fellow Prophets of the provinces.[20] This cannot yet be fully established on the basis of the evidence now available. But the question certainly deserves further study.

That oral documents were transmitted in ancient Israel, generation after generation, for centuries during the Pharisaic and Rabbinic period, has long been recognised. Neither the Mishna nor the Talmud nor the Tannaitic commentaries on the Pentateuch were put into writing before the sixth century C.E.[21] Yet the Mishna was *edited* as an oral document, and put into practically its present form early in the third century C.E., while the Tannaitic *midrashim* preserve passages which no one doubts were composed before the time of the Maccabees.[22]

The argument in the present volume merely indicates that this period of oral transmission for some documents was considerably longer than had hitherto been supposed. Parts of the Tannaitic *Midrashim* and some of the earliest passages of the Mishna and the *Tosefta* were transmitted orally, not for seven or eight centuries, but for twelve or thirteen centuries.

The significance of these ancient documents for a study of biblical exegesis and philology must be left to specialists in those fields. This book shares with the reader the results of an inquiry which, after some years of hesitation, I now submit to the world of scholarship for appraisal.

CHAPTER II

THE EXILIC ORIGIN OF
SIFRE DEUTERONOMY 342

In *Sifre* Deuteronomy 342 (p. 391), a passage has been preserved which, it can be shown, was composed not later than the early years of the Babylonian Exile, and perhaps in the last decades of the First Commonwealth.

The passage asserts that Moses gave his blessing to the people before his death because at an earlier time "he had spoken harsh words" to them. Having reproved them severely, he was impelled at the end to part from them with gentle words of comfort and consolation. "And," continues *Sifre,* " *'all'* the Prophets learned from him, at first addressing harsh words to Israel, but in the end turning about and speaking words of consolation." *Sifre* cites as examples: Hosea, Joel, Amos, Micah, and Jeremiah.

With the exception of Joel and Jeremiah, the verses of consolation quoted from the Prophets were the concluding verses of their Books, like those of Moses. However, the verses of consolation from Joel were not taken from the end of his Book but from the conclusion of Chapter 2: "And I will restore to you the years that the locust hath eaten . . ." (Joel 2.25). Similarly, the verses quoted from Jeremiah were taken not from Chapter 51 or 52 but from Chapter 31: "Then shall the virgin rejoice in the dance . . ." (Jer. 31.13 ff.).

In the extant text of *Sifre,* the homilist quotes a passage from Jeremiah 51.64 in this context: "Lest one infer that having offered them consolation, the Prophets reverted to reproof of them, Scripture says: 'Thus shall Babylon sink, and shall not rise again because of this evil that I will bring upon her. . . Thus far are the words of Jeremiah.' " It will be shown, however, that this passage was not part of the original homily; it was inserted in *Sifre* in consonance with

14

a comment of R. Johanan in *Yer. Berakot* 5.1, 8b. It there-fore does not bear on the present study.

Particularly because of the remark that this style characterized '*all*' the Prophets (this reading is found in all texts and versions of the homily), it is surprising that the two outstanding authors of such consolatory messages, viz. Isaiah and Ezekiel, were omitted from *Sifre*. The Talmud every-where accepts the unity of the Book of Isaiah. Regarded as a unit, that Book is the most obvious example of the style described in *Sifre*. The Book opens with an indictment of the people, and ends with a series of consolatory messages. Ezekiel's early prophecies also contain severe denunciations of the people, but his final chapters (37-48) were devoted to hopeful predictions.

It is apparent that the homilist, although specifically including *all* the Prophets in his generalisation, had in mind only the pre-Exilic ones. Because he flourished before their time, he omitted Ezekiel and the Second Isaiah. Indeed, that is how the authors of an ancient norm, preserved in *Tosefta Berakot* 3.21 (ed. Lieberman, p. 17), interpreted *Sifre*. The norm reads: "One may not rise to pray immediately after conversation, or play, or lightheadedness, but only after *words of wisdom*. Similarly, one ought not to part from a friend immediately after conversation, or play, or lightheadedness, but only after words of wisdom. For thus we find that *the early Prophets*[2] ended their messages with words of praise and comfort[3]." It can hardly be doubted that the halakist to whom we owe this rule had in mind the passage of *Sifre* under consideration. He did not say, however, that *all* the Prophets followed the indicated style; he imputed it only to the *early*, or pre-Exilic Prophets.

How the fact that the pre-Exilic Prophets closed their messages "with words of comfort and praise" could justify the later requirement that "words of wisdom" be used for parting messages and as preparation for prayer will be dis-cussed later (see p. 91). The implication of the norm seems to be that the consolatory passages at the end of the Pro-phetic Books were typical of the concluding words of each address. The Prophets uttered their words either just before prayer or just before leaving. In either event, the halakist assumed that they concluded their addresses with words of comfort and consolation, just as their Books end with such words. Apparently, the Prophetic teachers were known to have formulated their messages in these early times at assemblies which ended in prayer. Because of this, the halakist taught further that anyone parting from a neighbour should include "words of wisdom" in his parting remarks. This teaching applied particularly to preparation for the final parting from the world. That is why Moses, whose example was followed by *all* the Prophets, gave his final blessing, according to the homilist, in words of comfort, encouragement, hope, and consolation.

Such an attitude was by no means universal. As *Sifre* Deuteronomy 1 (pp. 1 ff), shows (see p. 19), other homilists held that one's last words should be words of rebuke. They maintained that this rule was followed by Jacob, whose "blessing" of his sons was, in their opinion, a series of rebukes. The same rule, according to these homilists, was adopted by Moses, David, Jeremiah, and others. Obviously both the authors of *Sifre* Deuteronomy 342 (p. 391), and of the norm under consideration, disagreed with the teachings of Sifre Deuteronomy 1.

While the passage in *Sifre* Deuteronomy 342 dates at the latest from the Exile, the norm based on it was apparently composed during the early years of the Restoration. Its author distinguished the "early Prophets," who flourished before the Exile, from the later ones of his own generation. Knowing that the authors of the passage in *Sifre* from which he drew his inference had lived during the Exile, he interpreted the term "all the Prophets" in *Sifre* to mean the pre-Exilic ones. The normist could not say that *all* the Prophets ended their remarks with words of consolation, because he could not be sure it would be true of the Prophets who were his contemporaries or their successors.

However, the question remains: Why did the author of the passage in *Sifre* quote the final verse of Joel, Chapter 2, as the closing remarks of the Prophet? Revisers of the homily, whose work has been preserved in *Midrash Tannaim*[4] (hereafter *M*), recognised this difficulty and substituted for the verses quoted in *Sifre* from Joel, Chapter 2, those which occur at the end of the Book. The same change was made by the author of *Pesiqta Zutreta,* who may either have made the identical emendation on his own initiative or relied on the version of *M.* The emendation of the revisers only emphasizes the fact that *Sifre* itself did not quote the fourth chapter of Joel, but the second. A natural explanation of the homilist's citation of Chapter 2, instead of Chapter 4, may be that he regarded the former as the end of Joel's first prophecy, dealing with the locusts. The final two chapters of Joel deal with the eschatological future and did not concern the homilist.

But it is also possible that the homilist of *Sifre* knew the Book of Joel in an early version containing only what are now its first two chapters. In that event, we must assume that the latter half of the Book was composed by an anonymous Prophet and was combined with the original Book of Joel because of its brevity. That combinations of this type were common under such circumstances is definitely asserted by the later Talmudists, who doubtless had a firm tradition to this effect.[5]

Similarly, the homilist's quotation of the consolatory passage in Jeremiah, Chapter 31, suggests that in his time that chapter marked the end of the Prophetic Book. Even in a later generation, what is now the Book of Jeremiah constituted two separate treatises, as is shown below (see p. 21). Of those treatises, the first ended with what is now Chapter 31. It was the book described in Jeremiah, Chapter 36, where the Prophet was commanded to inscribe in a scroll all the messages he had uttered from the beginning until that time, the fourth year of the reign of King Jehoiakim. After King Jehoiakim burned the scroll, the Prophet drew up another copy of the treatise (Jer. 36.32) with some supplements. The second work was a collection of the prophecies of Jeremiah delivered after the composition of the first scroll. It therefore included all the speeches the Prophet delivered during the reign of King Zedekiah and in Egypt near the end of his life. The deportees to Babylonia in 597 B.C.E. could know only the first treatise of Jeremiah. The homilist, being one of them, therefore considered Chapter 31 the concluding chapter of the Book of Jeremiah. The halakist, although

17

he lived after the Restoration and therefore knew both parts of Jeremiah, understood the significance of the homilist's remark and interpreted it correctly.

It must still be asked, however, why the homilist in *Sifre* overlooked the Book of Isaiah. Granted that the homilist lived during the Exile, before the Second Isaiah, why did he fail to mention the First Isaiah? If he considered the final prophecies of the First Isaiah consolatory, he should have mentioned that fact. If, on the other hand, he interpreted them as words of admonition, why did he say that *all* the Prophets followed the style set by Moses?

Apparently, he did not mention the First Isaiah because at the time that Prophet seemed to have been repudiated by the course of events. Isaiah, alone among the true Prophets, had held Zion to be inviolable. And, indeed, his predictions proved true in his day. But the exiles in Babylonia might well reject him as a Prophet, in view of what had happened to them.

From this examination, it appears highly probable, if not certain, that the homily under consideration was composed by one of the exiles in Babylonia who had been deported with King Jehoiachin in the year 597 B.C.E.

CHAPTER III

THE EXILIC ORIGIN OF A SECTION OF *SIFRE* DEUTERONOMY 1

Sifre Deuteronomy 1 contains at least one section which was composed by a homilist who flourished during the early years of the Exile. He may have been acquainted with the homily discussed in the preceding chapter. In any event, he lived at a somewhat later period. The date may be determined by the state of the canonical works in his time. Like the homilist of *Sifre* Deuteronomy 342 (p. 392),[1] he had a Book of Jeremiah which ended with Chapter 31; but unlike that homilist, he also knew of another Book of Jeremiah, containing what are now Chapters 32 to 51.[2] He still did not recognize the Psalms as a canonical work,[3] nor did he know the concluding chapters of Proverbs. Perhaps he did not know of Proverbs at all; at least not as a sacred book.[4] He possessed oral traditions which he could trace back to the Prophet Amos, who, according to him, "prophesied more than all his colleagues." His text of the Book of Samuel did not yet contain the Song of David, which now constitutes Chapter 22. He considered the Book of Deuteronomy a work of reproof and rebuke to Israel by Moses, and took issue with the doctrine of *Sifre* Deuteronomy 342 (p. 392), which held that Moses, like all the other Prophets, ended his career with words of consolation to Israel.[5]

All this is clearly implied in the very first section of the homilist's work. Only through radical emendation has it been possible for commentators and copyists to conceal from themselves the early date of the treatise, which was in fact composed long before the time of the Men of the Great Synagogue, and probably before the Restoration.

The treatise opens with a comment on the very first phrase of Deuteronomy: "These are the words which Moses spoke." The homilist asks: "Did Moses prophesy only these words? Did he not write the whole Torah, as it is said, 'And Moses wrote this Torah' (Deut. 31.9)? Why then does Scripture say, *'These* are the words which Moses spoke'? The verse teaches us that these were words of admonition, as it is said, 'But Jeshurun waxed fat and kicked' (Deut. 32.15)."

Sifre continues, citing other works which begin either with "These are the words," or a similar expression, maintaining that the implication in each instance is that what follows constitutes reproof and admonition. Thus, the Book of Amos, beginning with "The words of Amos," consists of seven indictments of Israel. *Sifre* also asserts that we must explain the verse, Jeremiah 30.4, which reads: "And these are the words which Jeremiah[6] spoke concerning Israel and concerning Judah." *Sifre* asks: "Did Jeremiah prophesy only these words? Did not Jeremiah write *two* Books, as it is said, 'Thus far are the words of Jeremiah' (Jer. 51.64)? Why then does the verse quoted say, 'And *these are* the words, etc.' The words tell us that the message was a reproof."

Sifre goes on to quote II Samuel 23.1, which reads: "Now *these* are the last words of David." Here also *Sifre* asks: "Did David prophesy only these words? Does not Scripture continue, 'The spirit of the Lord spoke by me, and His word was upon my tongue' (*ibid.*)?" The homilist takes this verse to mean that David had "prophesied" other messages as well as the one cited in the chapter under consideration. "Why, then," continues *Sifre,* "does Scripture say, 'And these are the last words of David?' Because they were words of reproof. And whence do we know that they were words of reproof? Because Scripture continues: 'But the ungodly, they are as thorns thrust away, all of them, for they cannot be taken with the hand' (II Sam. 23.6)."

This text has puzzled the commentators. Was it the contention of the author that the whole Book of Deuteronomy consisted only of reproofs? That appears impossible, for a large part of the Book contains normative law. Because of this difficulty, Rashi (Deut. 1.1), paraphrasing the *baraita* of *Sifre,* cites as examples of the "reproof" only verses from the very first chapter of Deuteronomy. But, as already noted, *Sifre* itself draws its example from Deuteronomy, Chapter 32. The purpose of the quotation from one of the final chapters seems to be to stress the view that the whole Book consisted of reproofs.

It seemed equally difficult to understand the author's remark that Jeremiah wrote two Books, and his quoting as evidence the concluding verse of Jeremiah, Chapter 51. It is true that, according to the Talmud,[7] Jeremiah wrote three Books: the one bearing his name, the Book of Kings, and Lamentations. The homilist in *Sifre* might conceivably have ascribed to Jeremiah the Book bearing his name and only one other; but how could he establish this ascription from the final verse of Jeremiah, Chapter 51? No less perplexing is the homilist's failure to comment on the title of the Book, "The words of Jeremiah."

The homilist demonstrated that King David "prophesied" more than the few verses of II Samuel, Chapter 23, by quoting a remark from that very chapter; but why did he not mention the Book of Psalms, or at least those parts of it which are expressly ascribed to David? Moreover, he did not even refer to II Samuel, Chapter 22, which now contains the Song of David. Why did he rely on an indirect suggestion that David spoke other messages of prophecy, when one was included in the historical Books of the Prophets? Why did he make no mention of the final chapters of Proverbs, which begin with such phrases as "The words of Agur, the son of Jakeh" (Prov. 30.1) and "The words of King Lemuel" (*ibid.* 31.1)? What did the homilist mean by the remark that Amos prophesied "more than all his colleagues"?[8] (In my edition of *Sifre* Deuteronomy, I erroneously adopted the reading of Ms. Berlin and *Yalkut ha-Makiri* for this passage, *viz.* "Did Amos prophesy only these words? Did he not prophesy regarding more [nations] than all his colleagues?" However, all the other codices and *ed. pr.* read simply, "Did he not prophesy *more than* all his colleagues," and doubtless that is the correct reading. The reading of Ms. Berlin and *Yalkut ha-Makiri* represents only an effort by a Spanish copyist to overcome the textual difficulties.)

The Book of Amos is in fact smaller than the works of either Isaiah or Hosea, both of whom prophesied at approximately the same time as he and might, therefore, be called his colleagues. Moreover, *Sifre* was commenting on the heading of the Book of Amos, indicating that *these* were his only prophecies. The clear implication of the remark is that the homilist knew of other prophecies by Amos not included in the Book. Once we recognize that the homilist flourished during the Exile, the difficulties disappear. He was referring to the various parts of the Bible as he knew them. In his time, the first verse of the present Book of Jeremiah had not yet been added to the text. Therefore, the homilist had to cite Jeremiah 30.4 to raise the question of why the words, "These are the words of Jeremiah," were used to describe Chapters 30-31, when in fact, the Prophet had composed two treatises. As already noted, his text of the Book of Samuel did not yet include Chapter 22, containing the Song of David.

It is difficult to believe that a homilist living after the Exile, had so primitive a text of the Scriptures. It is equally difficult to believe that at that period he could still possess *oral* teachings going back to the Prophet Amos. On the other hand, the homilist seems to have been acquainted with *Sifre* on Deuteronomy 33, and to have taken issue with it. His emphatic assertion that Moses' final words to Israel were rebukes and admonitions, seems to be directed against the view that the Prophets, following the example of Moses, concluded their careers with words of comfort to the people.[9] Naturally, the passage has been changed and greatly augmented during the twenty-six centuries since it was composed.

Thus, after the discussion of the meaning of the expressions, "The words of" and "These are the words of," when used as headings for Books or chapters, *Sifre* Deuteronomy 1 (p. 2) says: "Similarly, we read, 'The words of Koheleth, the son of David, king in Jerusalem' (Eccl. 1.1). But did Solomon prophesy[10] only this Book? Did he not write three Books, while half of his wisdom was expressed in parables? Why then does Scripture read: 'The words of Koheleth'? This teaches us that they were words of reproof." As the sanctity of the Book of Ecclesiastes was still under dispute after the destruction of the Second Temple,[11] this passage probably did not derive from the Exilic homilist. It was added by a glossator who remembered that Ecclesiastes, too, began with "The words of. . . ."

From all this evidence, it seems patent that this part of *Sifre* Deuteronomy 1, and perhaps other comments found in this opening portion of *Sifre* Deuteronomy, were composed during the Exile. Like the portion of *Sifre* discussed in the preceding chapter, this homily was composed by a Prophet or a member of the Prophetic school who, as we have observed, had access not only to the written books of the Prophetic canon, as it was then constituted, but to oral traditions stemming from pre-Exilic Prophets. These may have been forgotten in the centuries which have elapsed since that time; or they may have become part of the Pharisaic and Rabbinic tradition preserved in the Talmud and *Midrashim*.

CHAPTER IV

THE PROPHETIC ORIGIN OF A
HOMILY IN *SIFRE* DEUTERONOMY 48

Commenting on the verse, "For if ye shall diligently keep all this commandment which I command you, to do it, to love the Lord your God, to walk in all His ways, and to cleave unto Him, then will the Lord drive out all these nations from before you . . ." (Deut. 11.22,23), *Sifre* Deuteronomy 48 (p. 112) interprets the word *shamar* ("to keep") as to preserve, teach, and study, as it is frequently interpreted in various *Midrashim*.[1]

Hence *Sifre* states: "Lest you say, 'Let the children of the elders study, let the children of the great men study, *let the children of the Prophets* study [the Commandments],' therefore Scripture warns 'For if ye shall diligently *keep* [according to this interpretation, *preserve*] this commandment, which I command you, to do it, to love the Lord your God, to walk in all His ways, and to cleave unto Him (Deut. 11.22)'. This teaches us that all are alike in their relation to the Torah. And thus Scripture says further, 'Moses commanded us a Torah, an inheritance of the congregation of Jacob (*ibid*. 33.4)'. Scripture does not say [an inheritance of] the priests, the Levites, or the Israelites, but the community of Jacob. And similarly Scripture says, 'Ye are standing this day *all of you* before the Lord your God (*ibid*., 29.9)'. Were it not for this one man, who arose and preserved (*qiyyem*) the Torah, would it not have been forgotten?" In explanation of the last phrase, a glossator added: "Had not Shaphan [II Kings 22.8 ff.] arisen in his time, Ezra in his time, R. Akiba in his time, would not the Torah have been forgotten? And thus Scripture says, 'And a word in due season, how good is it!' (Prov. 15.23). The word which this one person spoke outweighs all else."

The core of the homily certainly implies that its author's

contemporaries were Prophets. An ordinary Israelite, unwilling to devote himself to the study of Torah, might be expected to take refuge in the claim that it would be preserved by the Prophetic schools, or the children of the Elders, or the children of the powerful. No one living after the cessation of Prophecy would have been likely to mention the children or disciples of the Prophets in this context.

If the text had been composed in the post-Prophetic age, we would have expected it to read, "children of the Sages" instead of "children of the Prophets"; for a person who was not the child of a scholar might well demand that the burden of preserving the Torah be placed on children of scholars. Yet the reading "children of the Prophets" is attested by all the extant texts, and is doubtless authentic. We can only conclude that this comment was composed in the Prophetic schools. Whether this was before the Exile, during the Exile, or after the Exile, cannot be determined.

CHAPTER V

THE PROPHETIC ORIGIN OF A COMMENT IN *SIFRE* ON DEUTERONOMY 18.15

Sifre Deuteronomy 175 (p. 221) has preserved a comment on Deuteronomy 18.15, which must be of pre-Exilic origin. Deuteronomy 18.15 reads: "A Prophet will the Lord, thy God, raise up unto thee, from the midst of thee, of thy brethren, like unto me; unto him ye shall hearken."

Sifre interprets the word *meqirbeha* ("from the midst of thee") as follows: "And not from outside the Land of Israel." Evidently the authors of the passage knew nothing about Ezekiel, who prophesied in Babylonia. They could also not have been acquainted with the prophecies of Jeremiah in Egypt (Jer. 43.8 ff.), or the story of Jonah and his prophecies in Nineveh. It is clear, therefore, that this comment derives from teachers who lived before the fall of Jerusalem in 586 B.C.E.; and probably before the exile of Jehoiachin and many Judaites in 597 B.C.E.

Probably, the treatise of which this comment is a part, therefore, was composed in its earliest form in pre-Exilic times. How much of that original text survives in the present treatise cannot be definitely ascertained. But it is obvious from the text of *Sifre* that there were Israelites outside the land of Israel when this comment was composed. Presumably, the author was thinking of the people deported to Assyria, both those from Israel by Shalmaneser in 722 B.C.E., and those from Judah by Sennacherib during the reign of Hezekiah. He may also have had in mind the garrison of Israelites at Elephantine in Egypt; or communities which had found refuge in Ammon, Moab, Edom, and Phoenicia, as well as perhaps, Damascus.

The assertion that prophecy was limited to the land of Israel is apparently quoted in *Mekilta Bo*, Chapter 1 (p. 2), which states: "Before the Land of Israel was chosen, all countries were fit for prophecy. Once the Land of Israel was chosen, all other lands were excluded." *Mekilta* adds, however, "If you should argue from the Prophets with whom He spoke outside Israel, [the answer is] that although He spoke with them outside the Land of Israel, He spoke with them only because of the merit of the Patriarchs, as it is said, 'Thus saith the Lord: A voice is heard in Ramah. . . Thus saith the Lord: Refrain thy voice from weeping and thine eyes from tears; for thy work shall be rewarded, saith the Lord' (Jer. 31.15-16). And some say that although He spoke with them outside the Land, and for the sake of the Patriarchs, He spoke with them only in a pure place, on the water, as it is said, 'And I was by the stream Ulai' (Dan. 8.2), and it is said, 'as I was by the side of the great river, which is Tigris' (*ibid.* 10.4), and it is said, 'The word of the Lord came expressly unto Ezekiel the priest, the son of Buzi, in the land of the Chaldeans, by the river Chebar' (Ezek. 1.3). But others say, He spoke with him in the Land, and He spoke with him outside the Land."

The compilers of *Mekilta* made an effort to reconcile the norm of *Sifre* with the historical fact that Ezekiel did prophesy in Babylonia and Jeremiah in Egypt. The most natural suggestion was that once a person had become a Prophet in the Holy Land, he could also prophesy elsewhere. However, the transmitters of *Mekilta*, feeling that this was a forced explanation which did not account for Prophets who had never prophesied in the Holy Land and yet had prophesied outside it, suggested other explanations to meet the difficulty.

The authors of the Book of Daniel probably knew this passage of *Mekilta* in an earlier version, as well as that of *Sifre*. That is why, in fact, they insisted that Daniel saw his visions by the side of the river Tigris. Curiously enough, *Mekilta* does not explicitly raise the question of how it came about that Jeremiah prophesied in Egypt (Jer. 43.9; 44.1) or that Jonah heard the Divine word in Nineveh (Jonah 4.9).

We must assume that the original author of the passages in *Sifre* as well as *Mekilta* flourished before the Exile. That is why they knew nothing of Ezekiel, of the prophecies of Jeremiah in Egypt, or of the Book of Jonah. As the scene of the Book of Job is also placed outside the land of Israel

(Job 1.1), it seems obvious that these authors did not know the chapters (38ff.) in which God spoke to Job out of the whirlwind.

The date of the treatise in *Sifre* can be determined more precisely. *Sifre* (*loc. cit.*) comments on the phrases, "of thy brethren" and "unto thee" as follows: "*of thy brethren,* and not from others. *Unto thee,* and not for the Gentiles. How, then, shall we interpret the verse, 'I have appointed thee a Prophet unto the nations' (Jer. 1.5)? This verse refers to those who follow the ways of the Gentiles." It is uncertain whether the final sentence of this passage is original or not. It may well have been added by an editor in an effort to reconcile the homilist's comment with the statement of Jeremiah. However, it is evident that even the editor was unaware of the section in Jeremiah (46 ff.) beginning with "The word of the Lord came to Jeremiah the Prophet concerning the nations" (*ibid.* 46.1). Neither the author nor the editor could have been aware of the similar prophecies in Isaiah (13-21) or Ezekiel (25-32; 35). They could have had no knowledge of the Book of Jonah, wherein Jonah was expressly sent to prophesy to the people of Nineveh (Jonah 1.2; 3.2); or of the Books of Obadiah (1.1); or Nahum, which is headed "The burden of Nineveh" (Nah. 1.1).

On the other hand, the prophecies in Amos, Chapters 1 and 2, are quite consistent with the doctrine of *Sifre*. Amos predicts the downfall of the various nations he mentions, but he does so only in an introduction to his denunciation of Israel (Amos 2.6). His purpose in enumerating the transgressions of the various nations and describing their downfall, was to stress their equality before God with Israel itself. God holds them accountable for their transgressions, precisely as he does Israel. Amos, of course, returns to emphasize the equality of the Gentiles with the Israelites before God: "Are ye not as the children of the Ethiopians unto me, O children of Israel?" (Amos 9.7).

Thus, the author of the comment in *Sifre* on Deuteronomy 18.15 certainly flourished before the time of Nahum as well as before that of Obadiah, the author of Jonah and Ezekiel. He antedated the flight of Jeremiah to Egypt, and the incorporation of Isaiah, Chapters 13 to 19, into the Book bearing that Prophet's name. That the author was also unacquainted with the Book of Job is evident, not only from the fact that according to that Book God talked to men outside the land of Israel, but from the fact that they were Gentiles, who, according to this passage of *Sifre,* could not be Prophets.

Later Jewish tradition reconciled the revelation of the Divine word to Job and Eliphaz with the statement of *Sifre* by insisting that they, like Balaam, were contemporary with Moses or even with the Patriarchs.[1] Despite this effort to reconcile the existence of Job, and the fact that the Divine word came to him, with the statement of *Sifre,* it seems obvious that the authors of the comment under consideration lived before the Book of Job was composed in its present form.

From what has been said it follows that the *terminus ad quem* for the composition of these passages of *Sifre* is the fall of Nineveh, or rather the denunciation of Nineveh by the Prophet Nahum. The *terminus a quo* remains to be determined. The passage from *Mekilta* may have been composed at a later time, perhaps during the Exile itself, by scholars who rejected Ezekiel's claim to prophecy.

The sections of *Sifre* considered in this chapter accordingly were composed at about the same time as the passage in *Sifre* Deuteronomy 342 (p. 391), discussed in Chapter 2 (see pp. 14 ff.). Both authors flourished before the final prophecies of Jeremiah had been uttered, and knew nothing about Ezekiel or the later Prophets of the Twelve. The author of *Sifre* Deuteronomy 175 did not regard Balaam as a Prophet, but as a wizard (Josh. 13.22). In this he disagreed with the *Sifre* Deuteronomy 357 (p. 430), where Balaam is described as a Prophet.

CHAPTER VI

A PROPHETIC COMMENTARY
ON THE DECALOGUE

There is evidence that, like the passages from *Sifre* Deuteronomy discussed in the preceding chapters,[1] the main body of *Mekilta* on the Decalogue was composed by Prophets. Possibly this early commentary on the Decalogue was part of an even larger Prophetic work, commenting also on Exodus. Chapters 21 to 23, *i.e.*, the whole Book of the Covenant. In this chapter, we can consider only one passage from the commentary on the Decalogue which seems obviously Prophetic in origin.

In the opening paragraphs of the Decalogue, God states that He shows mercy "unto the thousandth generation of them that love Me and keep (*shomré*) My commandments" (Exod. 20.6). *Mekilta Bahodesh* Chapter 6 (p. 227), identifies "them that love Me" as being "Abraham and those like him," while "(those who) keep My commandments," are identified as the Prophets. The ancient exegete could not, of course, mean that only the Prophets *observed* the commandments, or even that observance of the commandments was the main distinction of the Prophets. Clearly, he interpreted the verb *shamar* ("to keep") precisely as did the author of the passage cited above (p. 24) from *Sifre* Deuteronomy 48 (p. 112), to mean to study or preserve. He held that one of the primary duties of the Prophets was to study, teach, and preserve the Commandments. The comment was made by a contemporary of the Prophets, and before the rise of the intellectual leaders who came to be called "the Sages". For after the end of Prophecy, the persons responsible for the study and transmission of the Torah and its commandments were of course the "Sages of Israel."[2]

The doctrine declaring the Prophets the exponents and preservers of the Commandments, which is taken for granted in this comment, was proclaimed in an early version of Mishna *Abot* 1.1, also composed by the Prophets and their contemporaries. This will be demonstrated in Chapter 10 (pp. 77 ff.). From the beginning this doctrine was opposed by the Temple priests, who, as has been shown above, considered themselves the trustees and authorized transmitters and interpreters of Torah. Their views are preserved in *Mekilta of R. Simeon*.[3] In this work, the passage corresponding to that in *Mekilta* under consideration, defines *"them that love Me"* and "those who serve God out of love for Him; and *those who 'keep My commandments'* as those who 'serve Him out of fear.'"

The priestly groups, who thus revised the Prophetic comment still found in its original in *Mekilta*, rejected the doctrine that "keeping the commandments," meant study of the Torah. They held, with their successors of a later generation, that "keeping the Torah" meant *practicing* its commandments.[4] They opposed the view, apparently first proposed in the Prophetic schools and repeated generation after generation by their disciples, that the study of Torah was even more important than the practice of rituals. Hence, according to the priests, both the expression *"them that love Me,"* and *those who "keep My commandments,"* signified men devoted to the observance of rituals. But according to priestly groups, fear of God was superior to love for Him as a religious motivation.[5] Hence, they maintained in their revision of the passage of *Mekilta* that God's mercy would be shown to those who love Him, but more especially to those who fear Him.

The editors who introduced these changes in the text of the Prophetic comment may have lived during the Hasmonean period, perhaps during the persecutions of Antiochus. It was important at that time to stress at all costs the virtue of observance of the commandments. Thus, the transmitters took it upon themselves to rephrase the ancient commentary in accordance with their own views and predilections.

The Prophets are again mentioned as contemporaries in *Mekilta* on the verses immediately following the Decalogue. Scripture relates that the people, frightened by the terrifying events accompanying the Revelation on Mount Sinai, said to Moses: "Speak thou with us, and we will hear; but let not God speak with us, lest we die" (Exod. 20.16). *Mekilta* (p. 237) comments: "This verse teaches us that they did not have sufficient strength to receive more than the Ten Commandments, for Scripture says, 'If we hear the voice of the Lord our God any more, then we shall die' (Deut. 5.22), but 'Go thou near and hear' (*ibid*. v. 24). At that moment, they won the privilege to have Prophets arise among them." The corresponding passage in *Mekilta of R. Simeon* (p. 155) simply says, "Because of this [statement] they acquired the privilege of having Prophets appointed for them."

Prophecy, as conceived in these comments, differs widely from the concept in the Prophetic books. According to the comments, the Prophets resembled Moses, being essentially jurists and even lawgivers. Both *Mekilta* and *Mekilta of R. Simeon* emphasize this concept through quotations from Deuteronomy 18.15: "A prophet will the Lord thy God raise up unto thee, from the midst of thee, of thy brethren, like unto me; unto him ye shall hearken." And, indeed, that verse is followed by the statement: "according to all that thou didst desire of the Lord thy God in Horeb, in the day of the assembly. . ." If this passage of *Mekilta* had derived from the era of the Sages, which followed that of the Prophets, it would doubtless have also mentioned the Sages as having the law-interpreting authority. Thus, the passage appears to derive from the time of the Prophets. Its notions are identical with those we will find in the document underlying the first Mishna of *Abot* and the beginning of ARN.[6]

CHAPTER VII

THE PROPHETIC AUTHORSHIP OF PASSAGES IN *SIFRE* DEUTERONOMY 310 and 313

In its comment on Deuteronomy 32.7, "Ask thy father, and he will declare unto thee thine elders, and they will tell thee," *Sifre* holds that "thy father" meant the Prophets; while "thine elders" was to be taken literally, signifying the aristocratic leadership of the community: "as it is said, 'Gather unto Me seventy men of the elders of Israel' (Num. 11.16)."[1]

As already observed (above, p. 16), *Midrash ha-Gadol* has preserved a revised version of *Sifre* on Deuteronomy, published under the title *Midrash Tannaim* by D. Z. Hoffmann. The authors of this version (to which we refer as M in this book), rejected (p. 189) the interpretation of *Sifre;* according to them, "the Elders" are to be identified with "the Sages." Clearly the reading of *Sifre* is the more ancient, dating from a time when the Elders, by unanimous agreement, played an important role in the religious life of the community. The revised version was composed when the Sages claimed the right to replace the Elders. The revisers did not reject the identification of "thy father" with "the Prophets." Yet it seems most unlikely that if the author of this passage in *Sifre* had lived after the end of prophecy, he would have given this interpretation to the term "thy father." He would probably have interpreted the word to correspond to a contemporary institution. It therefore seems that this passage, too, was composed in the era of the Prophets.

Similarly, another passage in *Sifre* on Deuteronomy (32.10) mentioning the Prophets, was probably composed by the Prophetic transmitters during the Exile or immediately after it. The passage interprets the verse as though it were a prediction of the future. "He *will find* him in a desert land, and in the waste, a howling wilderness; He *will encompass* him about; He will grant him understanding.[2] He *will keep* him as the apple of His eye." *Sifre* says: *"He will find him in a desert land*. This verse applies to the destined future, as it is said, 'Therefore, behold, I will allure her, and bring her into the wilderness, and speak tenderly unto her' (Hosea 2.16). *And in the waste, a howling wilderness*. This refers to the kingdoms,[3] as it is said, 'Who led thee through the great and dreadful wilderness' (Deut. 8.15). *He will encompass him him about*, with the Elders. *He will grant him understanding*, through the Prophets. *He will keep him as the apple of His eye*, as it is said, 'Surely, he that toucheth you toucheth the apple of His eye' (Zech. 2.12.)"[4] (In the extant texts of *Sifre*, the verse from Zechariah is preceded by the comment "He will protect them from the demons that they may not harm them." But these words are lacking in the corresponding passages in *M* (p. 192). There they are added to another homily, to which they doubtless belong.)

If the citation from Zechariah is original, the passage dates from the time of the Restoration. Again, it is significant that the authors of the revised version preserved in *M* changed the text to read: *"He will encompass him*, with Prophets; *He will grant him understanding*, through the *Sages*."[5] The authors of the revised version no longer knew of the Prophets as teachers; but they did identify their scholars as such. On the other hand, as we have seen, they saw no need for finding any reference in the Mosaic admonition to the Elders of their day.

The "kingdoms" to which the homilist refers were unrelated to the "four kingdoms" of Daniel's vision. The verse from Deuteronomy cited shows that the kingdoms were those through which the Israelites would have to pass in order to reach the Promised Land.

Once more the text of the revised version shows that in the Sopheric times, as we should expect, there was objection to paying homage to the "Elders"; and in their place the teachers mentioned "the Sages." It follows that the text of *Sifre*, which makes the Prophets those through whom understanding is granted the people and which still recognizes the role of the Elders, probably derives from the Exilic period, if not earlier.

CHAPTER VIII

THE PRE-EXILIC ORIGIN OF THE EARLIEST VERSION OF THE CENTRAL SYNAGOGUE PRAYER, THE 'AMIDAH

That the Prophets led prayer gatherings during Exilic and even in pre-Exilic times can definitely be established.[1] Ezekiel speaks of people who came to him "to inquire of the Lord" (20.1). On other occasions, he mentions the Elders of the community who "sat before me." (8.1; 14.1). The context shows that they had not come merely to visit him or to inquire about the future; they had come to ask him to pray on their own behalf or on behalf of the Holy City. His prayer is not quoted; perhaps it was a standard prayer, which did not need to be cited. He preserved only his own remarks on these occasions.

Jeremiah 14.7 ff. quotes a prayer offered by the Prophet on behalf of the people. In 14.11, Jeremiah was told not to intercede on their behalf. Again in 14.19 ff., he prayed for them; but in 15.1 ff., he was warned that not even Moses or Samuel could effectively intercede on their behalf. The Prophet was commanded to dismiss the gathering which, presumably, was in his house. Jeremiah's reference to Moses and Samuel suggests that it was part of the role of the Prophet to pray on behalf of the people. This role is assigned to Samuel again in Psalm 99.6. Similarly, according to Psalm 106.23, Moses stood in the breach, doubtless through his prayers, recorded in Exodus 32.11 ff., preventing the destruction of Israel. According to Psalm 106.30, Phineas offered such a prayer in the incident recorded in Numbers 25.1 ff. (see *ibid.* v. 11).

Correct interpretation of the various passages under consideration has been impeded only by the failure of some modern commentators to take into account two significant points: first, the urgent need of the Israelite community to engage in worship; and second, the impossibility of such

35

worship for the Prophetic following in the Temple of Jerusalem when it was defiled, or in the provincial sanctuaries, which were often led by renegade priests.

The defilement of the Temple by King Manasseh was doubtless as grave an event for the Prophetic following in his time, as the persecutions of Antiochus IV were in his day,[2] and those of Hadrian in his.[3] We know that both latter events left a permanent stamp on Jewish worship. It seems more than probable that the inevitable exclusion of the pious traditionalists from the Temple, because of its defilement by King Manasseh, involved the development of a prayer service, beyond what had been customary in earlier times.

Even if these Prophets had not alluded to such gatherings, we would be obliged to assume their existence. Surely, in the time of Ezekiel, some method of worship was provided for the people. They could not offer sacrifice away from Jerusalem; even those Judaites who may have rejected the doctrine of the centralisation of worship would have refrained from performing any sacred ritual in an "unclean land." The men who came to the Prophet, as indicated in Ezekiel 33.30 ff., assembled not only to hear his words of reproof; they came to request prayer on their behalf.

For a period in Jeremiah's career, he, too, must have served as a leader of the Prophetic following in prayer services. His career as a Prophet began in the thirteenth year of King Josiah's reign (Jer. 1.2). But the purification of the Temple did not occur until five years later (II Kgs. 22.3). How did the pious people, who rejected the idolatry introduced into the Temple by Manasseh, worship during this period; and indeed in the earlier generations after Manasseh had become a renegade? That they did not worship at all is inconceivable. The most pious of the people could not have refrained from communion with God.

They could not worship at the desecrated Temple, nor at the "high places" away from the Temple. Doubtless, some gathered to hear the worship of the Levites, who recited Psalms. But the Book of Jeremiah leaves no doubt that the Prophet was considered, even by those who had little faith in his effectiveness in predicting the future, a person who could pray on their behalf. Thus Zedekiah sent a delegation to him when Nebuchadnezzar was approaching, asking the Prophet to pray on behalf of the people (Jer. 21. 1.2).

We must not be misled by the Prophet's denunciation of the congregations who came to hear him. These were, for the most part, his supporters. But, like other orators, he spoke to them words really addressed to his opponents.

Long before the times of Jeremiah and Ezekiel, however, we hear of people visiting the Prophets on Sabbaths and New Moons (II Kgs. 4.23). It is difficult to assume that these were simply "visits," unrelated to worship.

Although we must have assumed, *a priori,* the existence of Prophetic prayer gatherings during the period when the faithful, monotheistic, antipriestly groups were forming in Judah and Israel, demonstration of the fact required unmistakable textual evidence. This can now be provided through study of a passage in *Sifre* Deuteronomy which has long been misunderstood. According to *Sifre* Deuteronomy 343 (pp. 394 ff.), the *'amidah,* now the central prayer of the synagogue service, was composed, in its earliest version, by "the early Prophets." We have already observed (p. 15) that the term "early Prophets" always means "pre-Exilic Prophets." The passage in *Sifre* containing this information was itself composed during the Exile. Its authors state that the *'amidah,* in the form in which it is quoted by them, had been formulated by early i.e. pre-Exilic Prophets. As we shall see, the time of the composition of this early prayer was probably long before the fall of Jerusalem in the year 586 B.C.E.

The passage under consideration is *Sifre* Deuteronomy 343 (pp. 394 ff.), which quotes an early form of the *'amidah.* It is a comment on Deuteronomy 33.2, "And he said: The Lord came from Sinai, and rose from Seir unto them; He shined forth from Mount Paran, and He came from *Ribbebot Qodesh.*"[4]

Sifre comments: "This verse teaches that Moses did not begin with the concerns of Israel before he began with the praise of God. His style may be compared to that of an advocate (*"rhetor"*) proceeding to his pulpit, having been hired[5] by someone to speak for him[6]. He [the advocate] did not begin with the concerns of that man [the client], before speaking the praise of the King. 'Happy is the world,[7] considering who is its King.[8] Happy is the world,[9] considering who is its judge.[10] The sun has shone upon us. The moon has shone upon us.' Then everyone[11] hailed the King with him. After that, he began with the concern of that man [the client]. And finally, he ended with praise of the King. Similarly, Moses did not begin with the concerns of Israel, before he began with the praise of God, as it is said, 'And he said: The Lord came from Sinai.' Then he began with the concerns of Israel: 'And there was a King in Jeshurun' (Deut. 33.5). And he concluded with the praise of God: 'There is none like unto God, O Jeshurun' (Deut. 33.26).

"So also King David began [his Psalm] with the praise of God, 'Hallelujah. Sing unto the Lord a new song' (Ps. 149.1). Then he turned to the *praise of*[12] *Israel,* 'For the Lord taketh pleasure in His people' (*ibid*. v.4). And he concluded with the praise of God, 'Hallelujah. Praise God in His Sanctuary' (Ps. 150.1).

"So also his son, Solomon, spoke first the praise of God. 'There is no God like Thee in the heaven, or in the earth; who keepest covenant and mercy' (II Chron. 6.14). Then he spoke about Israel: 'If there be in the land famine' (*ibid*. v. 28). He ended with the praise of God. 'Now, therefore, arise, O Lord, God, into Thy resting-place' (*ibid*. v. 41). And similarly in the eighteen benedictions,[13] which the *early* [or *the earliest*] Prophets[14] ordained that the people of Israel should pray,[15] they did not begin with the concerns of Israel before they began with the praise of God, 'the great, the mighty, and the awesome God';[16] and after that, 'Who releasest the captives';[17] and after that, 'Who healest the sick'; and *Modim*."[18] (For the meaning of this word, see below p. 126).

A recension of this homily, differing from that of *Sifre,* has been preserved in *M* (pp. 208 ff.). The variations between that recension and the text of *Sifre* are so great that they must be studied separately (see below, p. 40), and only a few, shedding light on the original reading of *Sifre,* can be considered here.

The present reading of the homily, as found in the various texts of *Sifre,* was obviously composed in the period of the Hellenistic, or more probably the Roman, domination of

Judea. The mention of the *rhetor* alone establishes this fact. The institution of the *rhetor,* the advocate of the accused client, and the Greek name for the office, imply Hellenistic influence. Indeed, the parable probably describes an actual occurrence witnessed by the editor. That is why the passage reports the advocate's plea in the past tense. Had the story been fictional, drawing on general experience and not on a specific instance, the historical present would have been more appropriate. Hence, too, the addition of the irrelevant comment that, hearing the advocate's praise, "everyone hailed the King." the king and the judge. The author vividly recalled the courtroom scene and was carried away by his memories of it. The word *meqallesim* ("hailed"), also deriving from the Greek, refers to the Roman custom of hailing Caesar.[19]

Flourishing at a late date, the editor of the homily in its present form readily quoted Psalms 149 and 150, as well as the Book of Chronicles. However, there is ample evidence that the original homily was much shorter and simpler. It contained only the statement that Moses, before discussing the needs of Israel, offered praise to God. It continued with the statement that the Prophets, who formulated the prescribed prayers, also began with the praise of God before they spoke of the needs of Israel. In this context, it quoted the usual prayer offered by the Prophets on behalf of the community—the prayer which ultimately developed into the synagogue *'amidah.*

It is evident that the rest of the extant homily was added to the original by later glossators and transmitters. Thus, Psalms 149 and 150 do not really illustrate the point which the homilist makes. For Psalm 149 contains no prayer for the needs of Israel; it speaks the praise of Israel. Indeed, in all the extant texts of *Sifre,* the phrase, "mention the concerns of Israel," found in the other parts of the homily, is replaced in this illustration with the words "with the praise of Israel." But how could a Psalm in which the praise of Israel followed the praise of God serve as an example of a liturgical style requiring praise of God before uttering a petition to Him? Even more importantly, the introduction to the homily asserted only that Moses did not wish to pray for Israel before extolling God; it said nothing about a requirement to conclude prayer with such praise. The necessity for concluding with praise of God occurs in the text only after the quotation of the parable of the *rhetor*. Apparently the addition was suggested by the example of the *rhetor*.

There is thus a fundamental difference in the liturgical style assumed in the opening comment and that predicated by the main body of the homily. This change in liturgical style is presumed in the illustrations drawn from Psalms 149, 150 and Chronicles. The *'amidah*, quoted as a composition of the early Prophets, provided (according to the reading of the *Sifre* in Ms. Berlin) no such concluding praise. The reading of that Ms. is surely to be accepted as authentic and original. But the word *u-modim,* found at the end of the *'amidah* cited in *Sifre* according to that text, does not refer to the prayer *modim 'anahnu lak,*[20] which is found in the *'amidah* according to all extant liturgies, and all the citations in the Rabbinic writings.

Had the word *u-modim* in *Sifre* referred to a final benediction extolling God, it would certainly have been preceded, as were all other quotations from the individual benedictions of the *'amidah,* with the phrase, "and after that." Yet the phrase is lacking not only in Ms. Berlin, but also in *Midrash Hakamim* and in the citation of this text by Rabbi Jacob of Sicily. It was also lacking in the text used by the revisers of the homily, who composed the corresponding passage in *M.*[21] It seems clear that the *u-modim* referred not to a benediction, such as is found in all extant liturgies toward the end of the *'amidah,* and beginning *modim 'anahnu lak* ("we acknowledge Thee"), but to a ceremony—the ceremony of prostration at the end of the *'amidah.* The root of the word *modim,* namely *ydh,*[22] means "prostration" in a number of passages, and doubtless has that connotation in the text under consideration.

Thus the citation from the *'amidah* in *Sifre* is to be translated: "And similarly in the (eighteen) benedictions which the early [or "earliest"] Prophets ordained that the people of Israel should pray, they did not begin with the concerns of Israel before they began with the praise of God, 'the great, the mighty, and the awesome God'; and after that, 'Who releasest the captives'; and after that, 'Who healest the

40

sick'; and they *prostrate* themselves." The custom of pros-
trating oneself at the end of the *'amidah* was still observed
when the recension of the homily, found in *M*, was composed.[23] However, to remind the congregation to observe this
ritual, the leader said the following words at the end of the
'amidah; "And now, our God, *modim 'anahnu lak"* (*i.e.*, we
prostrate ourselves before Thee). These words were a signal
for the congregation to perform the required ritual of
prostration, together with the leader.

From what has been said, it can be seen that neither
the author of the homily in *Sifre* nor the author of *M* were
acquainted with the blessings *Abodah*[24] and *Hodaah*,[25] or the
ceremony of the priestly benediction and the prayer for peace
which concludes the *'amidah* current in all extant rituals and
regularly cited in Rabbinic literature. The *'amidah*, as cited
in *Sifre*, could not, therefore, be described as *concluding* with
the *praise* of God. And indeed even the present text of *Sifre*
does not suggest that it did. While in the quotations of the
prayers of David and Solomon the final section is introduced
with the words, "And he returned and ended with the praise
of God," no such comment is made in regard to the *'amidah*.
Discussing the *'amidah*, *Sifre* simply states that the Prophets
"did not begin with the concerns of Israel, before they began
with the praise of God." Thus the original *Sifre* text under
consideration consisted only of two passages. The first
analysed the prayer of Moses in Deuteronomy 33; the second
cited the prayer of the Prophets in the *'amidah*. Both began
with the praise of God and afterward mentioned the needs
of Israel.

It was one of the theses of the treatise now incorporated
in this section of *Sifre* that the Prophets followed the example
of Moses. Thus, as we have seen (above p. 14), *Sifre* associated the consolatory endings of the Prophetic books with the
fact that Moses concluded his address to the Israelites in the
Book of Deuteronomy with the blessings of the tribes.[26] This
prayer, as analysed in this homily, followed a pattern common
in Scripture. Thus, Jacob finding himself in danger, prayed:
"God of my father, Abraham, and God of my father, Isaac, O
Lord, Who saidst unto me: Return unto thy country and to
thy kindred, and I will do thee good; I am not worthy of all

the mercies, and of all the truth, which thou hast shown unto Thy servant; for with my staff I passed over this Jordan; and now I am become two camps. Deliver me, I pray Thee, from the hand of my brother, from the hand of Esau, for I fear him. . ." (Gen. 32.10 ff.).

According to Deuteronomy, Moses followed this mode of prayer; so did King David (II Sam. 7.18 ff.; I Chron. 17.16 ff.) and King Solomon at the dedication of the Temple (I Kgs. 8.23 ff.). Even in the form cited in *Sifre* from II Chronicles (6.14 ff.) as an example of a prayer concluding with the concerns of God, King Solomon's prayer follows the usual style of Scripture. The final sentences, while appealing to God to dwell in Zion, were, in effect, petitions to Him on behalf of Israel. Following these examples, the prayer of Hezekiah in II Kings 19.15 ff. opened with the praise of God, and continued with a petition to Him (*ibid.* v. 16). The same style was adopted in the prayer ascribed to Moses in Psalm 90; in that of King David in I Chronicles 29.10 ff.; in that of Jeremiah in Jeremiah 32.17 ff.; in that of Nehemiah in Nehemiah 1.55 ff.; in that of the Covenant usually ascribed to the Great Synagogue (*ibid.* 9.6 ff.); and in that of Daniel in Daniel 9.4 ff.

It seems probable that the prayers ascribed to King David in I Chronicles 29.10 ff., as well as those of Nehemiah, the Men of the Great Synagogue, and Daniel, were actually influenced by the implied prescription of *Sifre,* according to the original form of the homily. This may also be true of the prayer ascribed to Hezekiah.

It is significant that in a number of these prayers (that of King David in II Samuel 7.25; that of King Solomon at the dedication of the Temple in I Kings 8.23; that of Hezekiah in II Kings 19.19; that of the Men of the Great Synagogue in Nehemiah 9.32; and that of Daniel in Daniel 9.15,17) the summation of the petitions is introduced with the word *ve-'attah* ("And now"). The identical style is followed in the prayers attributed to Mordecai and Esther in the Greek additions to the Book of Esther.[27] In those prayers, too, the transition from the words of praise to the petitions themselves is marked by the expression, "And now."

Although *Sifre,* even in its final form, cited only a few

benedictions of the 'amidah, its statement that the 'amidah contained "eighteen benedictions" led all the commentators to assume that those quoted were intended as examples selected at random. But this is highly improbable, for the following reasons. One of the benedictions quoted speaks of God as the One "Who releases the captives." Such a benediction is unknown in any other text of the 'amidah. (Various commentators and editors, including R. Elijah Gaon of Vilna, emending the text of the homily, have suggested that the phrase, "Who releases the captives," is a quotation from what is now the second benediction of the 'amidah. But in that benediction, this phrase follows the description of God as healer of the sick; whereas in *Sifre* the order is reversed.[28] *Sifre* could therefore not be quoting this benediction. Even more significantly, the texts of the second benediction of the *Genizah* do not contain any reference to "Who releases the captives" in the second benediction of the 'amidah. As these *Genizah* texts preserve the Palestinian form of the 'amidah, if *Sifre* had quoted the second benediction, it would have conformed to them. Therefore, we cannot take it that *Sifre*, citing God as the One "Who releases the captives," refers to the second benediction of the 'amidah. (See *J.Q.R.*, N.S. XVI, 1925, pp. 143-144.)

Finally, we cannot but assume that the homilist cited *all* the benedictions of the 'amidah current in his day. This is evident from *M* (as has been noted on p. 126, n. 21).

The homilist omitted the second benediction, including the affirmation of man's immortality and the resurrection of the dead; the petitions for wisdom, repentance, and forgiveness; the petitions for the ingathering of the exiles and the restoration of the Judges; and the final petition for peace. Indeed, *M* states categorically that "*At the end*, he says, 'And now, O Lord our God, we Thee prostrate ourselves before Thee.'" It follows that the authors of *M* did not yet know of the prayer for peace. Surely then, it was lacking in the early version of *Sifre*. But without the prayer for peace, the 'amidah does not contain eighteen benedictions. Therefore, the reading, "eighteen benedictions," cannot be original, and must have been introduced by a transmitter to replace another number. On the basis of the present texts, we cannot know what that number was, but there is no reason to assume that the benedictions cited were selected from a large *'amidah*. On the contrary, it would appear that the *'amidah* in the original homily contained only the benedictions mentioned. Hence, the homilist, introducing the successive petitions, said "and after that." The phrase can only mean "and *immediately* after that."

Thus the *'amidah* of *Sifre* as well as that of *M* antedated the establishment of the "eighteen benedictions," including some which, like the petition for Jerusalem, appear to be very ancient. But the date of the homilist of *Sifre* can be determined precisely. According to *Sifre,* the petition for the captives concluded with the doxology praising God as the One "Who releases the captives." The corresponding passage in *M* quotes, not the doxology of this prayer, but its opening petition; "Redeem us, O Lord our God, a *perfect redemption* from Thee." The substitution of this text for the doxology is significant. Presumably, the prayer had been revised by the time of *M*. It no longer spoke of "releasing the captives" but, as suggested by the petition, of "redeeming Israel." We may take it that by the time of the revisers, the doxology of this prayer was, as in the corresponding prayer of all versions (of the extant *'amidah*), "Blessed art Thou O Lord, the Redeemer of Israel."

The text of the *'amidah* was apparently altered when Israel was redeemed; *i.e.,* when Cyrus the Great permitted the exiles to return to the Holy Land. One could no longer pray for the release of the captives; they had been released. One could now pray only for *"a perfect redemption."* Feeling keenly the imperfection of the redemption under Cyrus, which fell far short of the glowing promises of Deutero-Isaiah, the people expressed their hopes for the future, even as they extolled God for the redemption of the present. As late as the proclamation of the Men of the Great Synagogue (Neh. 9.36), it was still asserted that the people were slaves on their own soil. Their predecessors, grateful for the permission to return to the land of Israel, still were concerned about the imperfection of their redemption. They prayed not only for a complete redemption but also stressed that it come "from Thee." The first redemption had come from Cyrus;

that was the reason for its inadequacy. The future one would come from God Himself.[29]

The revised *'amidah* of *M*, therefore, was composed soon after the Restoration. Perhaps the *'amidah* cited in *M* was actually changed in several stages, as will be suggested below. The first, immediately following the Restoration, required only an alteration in the prayer for the captives. Later, more basic changes, to be examined presently, were made. But if the *'amidah* quoted in *M* was the work of Prophets and Sages of the Restoration, the original homilist of *Sifre*, who knew only the earlier *'amidah*, must have flourished during the Exile. If so, the *'amidah* which he knew, and attributed to the early (or earliest) Prophets, was pre-Exilic. This is, of course, what we would expect from its ascription to "the early Prophets."

While the ascription of the origin of the *'amidah* to "the early (*i.e.*, pre-Exilic) Prophets" was later generally rejected by the scholars of Babylonia, and subsequently by the medieval commentators and codifiers and the modern historians of Judaism and the liturgy, it occurs several times in early Rabbinic literature. Thus in *Sifre* Numbers 42 (p. 46), R. Eleazar remarks: "Peace is great, as is evident from the fact that *the Prophets* planted only the idea of peace in the mouths of everyone." The commentators on *Sifre* have found this passage confusing and difficult. But it becomes clear, once we recognize that there was a continuing tradition, according to which the *'amidah* was in fact formulated by the Prophets. R. Eleazar knew this tradition. Perhaps, indeed, he knew the text of *Sifre* now under study. Hence he assumed that the *'amidah* of the Prophets contained the prayer for peace and therefore he says that they "planted peace in the mouths of everyone."

The tradition holding that the *'amidah* was formulated in pre-Exilic times underlies an interesting *baraita* quoted in *Tosefta Berakot* 3.6 (ed. Lieberman p.12; and see references there given). This *baraita* reads: "Lest you suppose that one is obliged to pray all day, it is explained in Daniel (6.11) 'And he kneeled upon his knees three times a day, and prayed, and gave thanks before his God.' Lest you think that he did this *only after he came into the Exile*, Scripture says, 'As he did aforetime.' " The authors of this *baraita* took it for granted that the prescribed prayers were recited in pre-Exilic times. (*Cf.* Professor Saul Lieberman in *Tosefta Kifeshutah, ad. loc.* pp. 29 ff.; and Professor Louis Ginzberg's *Commentary on the Yerushalmi* III, pp. 4 ff.). In *Mekilta* on Deuteronomy (12.5), published by Solomon Schechter from a *Genizah* Ms. in *Lewy Festschrift* (p. 191), the following comment occurs: " '[*But unto the place that the Lord your God shall choose out of all your tribes to put His name there*] *even unto His habitation shall ye seek.*' Because of this verse, the Prophets and the Elders ordained *to plant* in the mouths of Israel to pray thrice each day, saying: 'Restore Thy Presence to Zion and the order of Thy worship to Jerusalem Thy City.' "

The word *li-neto'a* ("to plant") has to be supplied in the Ms., for according to Schechter only the initial *lamed* can be made out in the Ms. But we may reasonably conjecture that the missing word was the one used in *Sifre* Numbers cited above, or a synonym of it. The exegete interprets the expression *leshikno* ("unto His habitation") as though it were an infinitive, "Ye shall seek that He may dwell." Thus the Prophets and the Elders prescribed that all the people should pray thrice each day that God may dwell (once more) in Zion.

But how could the liturgist pray during the Second Commonwealth for the *restoration* of the Divine Presence to Zion? Moreover, we know from the texts of the *Genizah* Mss.[30] that the prayer *Abodah*, of which the text in *Mekilta* on Deuteronomy is a variant, read in most synagogues in the Holy Land: "Do thou O Lord, our God, willingly dwell in Zion, Thy city, and may Thy servants worship Thee in Jerusalem." The text cited in *Mekilta* on Deuteronomy is also found in some citations,[31] but is much rarer than the alternative reading, which must have been formulated, and used, while the Temple still existed. We must therefore conclude that an editor of *Mekilta* on Deuteronomy, flourishing after the destruction of the Temple, substituted the text used in his community and in his time for that which had been cited originally in this work, and was ascribed to the Prophets. This was the usual formula mentioned above, "Do Thou O Lord, our God, willingly dwell in Zion, Thy city. . . ."

Therefore, according to *Mekilta* on Deuteronomy, precisely as according to *Sifre* Deuteronomy under consideration, the *'amidah* was originally composed by Prophets. The author of *Mekilta* ascribed to them the whole *'amidah* known in his day, while in *Sifre,* they are accurately portrayed as the authors of an original, germinal *'amidah.*

Both R. Eleazar (ben Shammua) and the anonymous author of the comment in *Mekilta* on Deuteronomy knew the *'amidah* in its fully developed later form. R. Eleazar lived long after the prayer for peace, unknown to the original homilist of *Sifre* Deuteronomy or the later transmitter, had been added to the *'amidah.* The *'amidah* of the time of the commentator in *Mekilta* on Deuteronomy contained the prayer for the Divine Presence in Jerusalem, likewise unmentioned in *Sifre* Deuteronomy. Their ascription of the authorship of the *'amidah* to the Prophets, however, unquestionably derived from older traditions; perhaps, indeed, from the homily in *Sifre.* Thus, their statements confirm the reading of *Sifre* found in Ms. Berlin and *Midrash Hakamim,* as contrasted with those found in the other texts of *Sifre.*

The concept of a pre-Exilic, Prophetic *'amidah* appears also to underlie the tradition according to which the prayer services of the synagogue were "established after the analogy of the daily sacrifices." This view is in one passage ascribed to R. Joshua ben Levi, (*B. Berakot* 26 b) but in *Yer. Berakot* 4.1,7 b, to his colleagues. R. Judah ben Ilai, some centuries earlier, took it for granted (*Tosefta Berakot* 3.1, ed. Lieberman p. 11). *Yer. Berakot, loc. cit.,* cites in support of R. Judah's view the *baraita* found in *Mekilta of R. Simeon* 16.21 (ed. Epstein-Melammed, p. 112), according to which the manna in the Wilderness melted at the end of the fourth hour after sunrise. *Yer.* ascribes to a tannaitic source the argument that this statement proves that morning ends with the fourth hour after sunrise and, therefore, morning prayers could not be said after that hour. If this was, indeed, R. Judah's view, his norm demanding that the morning prayers be said before the fourth hour would not reflect any relationship between the prayers and the Temple ritual.

None of these scholars could have been unaware of the

fact that regular prayers were said each day in the synagogue before the destruction of the Second Temple. Therefore, they could not mean that the *'amidah* had been established after the fall of Jerusalem in the time of Titus. Their comments must be taken to suggest that the *'amidah* was composed during the Babylonian Exile, because the departed Judaites could not offer sacrifices. But they could also mean that the prayer services were established during the reign of Ahaz or Manasseh, when the sacrifices could not properly be offered because of the pollution of the Temple under those kings.

In a very interesting and significant remark, R. Joshua ben Levi speaks of "those who established this prayer" (*Yer. Berakot* 2.4,4d). Seemingly, R. Joshua ben Levi knew the passage of *Sifre* under discussion. But he also knew of the widespread belief that the prayer services were established by the Men of the Great Synagogue. Unwilling to take sides in this controversy, he resorted to an ambiguity.

But if the early *'amidah* (as quoted in a document composed during the Babylonian Exile or shortly before it) was revised about the time of the Restoration under Cyrus, and was ascribed by the Exilic Prophets or their immediate predecessors to "the early (or earlier) Prophets," when was it composed? As the petition regarding the release of the captives indicates, this must have been at a time when many Judaites or Israelites were in captivity. This might have been the first Babylonian deportation in 597 B.C.E. More probably, it was in an earlier age, such as that of Hezekiah, when during the Assyrian war Sennacherib carried off more than 150,000 Judaites from their native land. On the first assumption, the term, "the early Prophets," refers to those before the first Exile. From the analogy of other passages, the term probably referred to Prophets of a much earlier age, and we may conclude that the *'amidah* in the early form cited in *Sifre* derived from contemporaries of Amos.

From the early Prophets the *'amidah* came to the Exilic and post-Exilic Prophets; from them to the Men of the Great Synagogue who embellished it greatly; from them to the Pharisees; and from the Pharisees to the Rabbis of the Talmud, and thus to our own time.

CHAPTER IX

THE PRE-EXILIC DOCUMENT
IN MISHNA *TA'ANIT* 4.2

One of the most fascinating documents of the Prophetic age surviving in Rabbinic literature is that preserved in Mishna *Ta'anit* 4.2. It can be demonstrated that the authors of that document flourished before the Exile and were probably Prophets who taught their tradition in their schools during the long period of suppression by King Manasseh, or during the last generations of the Second Commonwealth.

The document describes the division of the Holy Land into twenty-four regions, each responsible for the ministry at the Temple for two weeks a year—presumably one in the winter, the other in the summer. The system was probably established by Prophetic contemporaries of King Hezekiah, the king who abolished the "high places" or village altars (II Kgs. 18.22). The purpose of the document was to preserve the tradition established by King Hezekiah and his associates, declaring Jerusalem the sole Sanctuary of the whole land of Israel. At the same time it assured the adherents of Prophecy throughout the land an opportunity for local worship and arranged for their representation in Jerusalem in the national worship. It promised the priests of the local altars that they would be permitted to participate in the ministry at the Sanctuary in Jerusalem at least two weeks each year.

The Mishna reads: " 'Command the children of Israel and say unto them, My food which is presented unto Me [for offerings made by fire, of a sweet savour unto Me, shall ye observe to offer unto Me in due season]' (Num. 28.2).[1] How can a sacrifice be offered in the absence of the donor? Therefore the early Prophets [or "the earliest Prophets"][2] established twenty-four regions ["*mishmarot*"].[3] Each region ("*mishmar*") had a representation ["*ma'amad*"][4] of priests, Levites, and Israelites in Jerusalem. When the term of each region arrived, its priests and Levites went up to Jerusalem. The Israelites of the region gathered in their cities and recited the story of Creation. On the first day, they recited Genesis 1.1-8. On the second day, Genesis 1.6-12. On the third day, Genesis 1.9-18. On the fourth day, Genesis 1.13-23. On the fifth day, Genesis 1.20-31. On the sixth day 1.24-2.3. Large portions were divided among two readers, small portions were recited by one. In the morning, at the time of the additional sacrifice [on Sabbaths and festivals], in the afternoon, they recited [these portions] by heart as one recites the *Shema*."

Tosefta Ta'anit 3(4).2, (ed. Lieberman p. 337), implies a text of the Mishna which reads, not "the early Prophets," but "the Prophets of Jerusalem." *Tosefta,* after ascribing the establishment of the priestly and Levitical divisions to Moses, David, and Samuel the Seer, states that "the Prophets of Jerusalem arose and established twenty-four representations there [*i.e.*, in the Holy City] to correspond to the twenty-four *mishmarot* of the priesthood and Levitehood. For it is said, 'Command the children of Israel and say unto them, My food [which is presented unto Me] shall ye observe to offer Me in due season.' It is impossible to require all Israel [to be present at this daily sacrifice]. But this [verse] teaches us that an agent takes the place of his principal."

It is obvious that *Tosefta* offers a commentary on Mishna *Ta'anit* 4.2, explaining the necessity for the twenty-four representations in Jerusalem, and their nature, somewhat differently than is implied in the Mishna. The significance of the difference will become apparent below. However, had the authors of *Tosefta* read in their text of the Mishna "the early Prophets," doubtless they would have imputed the establishment of the twenty-four representations in Jerusalem to those authorities. *Tosefta* holds that the system was created by "the Prophets of Jerusalem," probably because they found that expression in the Mishna before them. Why the transmitters of the Mishna as now extant replaced the original "Prophets of Jerusalem" with "the early Prophets," will be made clear in the discussion below (p. 72).

The date of the composition of the Mishna can be established on the basis of the following data: (a) The use of the term *mishmarot* in the sense of geographical areas rather than of families, which it has everywhere else in Rabbinic literature; (b) the provision made in the Mishna for representations of priests and Levites in Jerusalem consisting of natives of the city; (c) the underlying concept of the Mishna that the daily sacrifice was offered on behalf of various regions of the country, each having a definite term assigned to it, rather than on behalf of the whole people— a concept unknown to the rest of the Talmud and clearly rejected in the Great Document of Nehemiah, Chapters 9-10; (d) the concept of the Mishna that the donor of a sacrifice should be present at the Temple at the time of its being offered by the priests—another concept virtually unknown to the rest of the Rabbinic tradition; (e) the doctrine that provincial priests and Levites could participate in the worship of the Temple of Jerusalem—a view contrary to the whole post-Exilic notion of the Temple ministry; (f) the chronological relation of the Mishna to (i) the Book of Chronicles, (ii) the records preserved in Ezra and Nehemiah, which go back to the period of the Restoration, and (iii) the record in *Tosefta Ta'anit* 3(4).2, which can itself be shown to antedate the Book of Chronicles. These data will be examined *seriatim* in this chapter.

A. The Meaning of the Term Mishmarot

In the Mishna under consideration, the word *mishmarot* cannot possibly signify anything but geographical areas. For the Mishna clearly states that when the time of a particular *Mishmar* came, *its* priests and Levites went up to Jerusalem, while the Israelites of the *mishmar* gathered in their cities for a local service. Clearly, the *mishmar* of the priests, Levites, and Israelites was the same. This could not be if *mishmar* meant "clan" or "family." If the word had had that meaning, the clan of priests would have no relation to the corresponding clan of Levites or to that of the Israelites.

Yet throughout Rabbinic literature, the *mishmarot* of the priests and the Levites were kinship groups. Thus, *Tosefta Ta'anit*, 2.1., (ed. Lieberman p. 328), states that "four *mishmarot* came up from the Exile: Jedaiah, Harim, Pashhur, and Immer." According to *Tosefta Ta'anit* 3(4).2, (ed. Lieberman p. 336), "Moses created eight *mishmarot* for the priesthood and eight for the Levitehood. When David and Samuel the Seer arose, they divided them into twenty-four *mishmarot* of the priesthood and twenty-four of the Levitehood." Clearly, the divisions made by these authorities were based on kinship. The *mishmarot* of the priests were numerically the same as those of the Levites; but one could not speak of the Levites and priests belonging to the same *mishmar*. And surely one did not think of Israelites as belonging to these *mishmarot*.

Why does Mishna *Ta'anit* use the term in the unique sense of geographical area? Because the Mishna under consideration was composed before the Exile, when the various groups of priests and Levites came from different regions of the country. They were not necessarily recognised as kinship groups before the Exile (see below, p. 53). Only during that period, did the priests and Levites who had been associated with one another in the ministry of their geographical areas come to regard one another as descended from the same ancestors. Such identification of regional background with kinship underlies a large part of the Book of Chronicles, where again and again the former inhabitants of particular localities are described as descendants of eponyms, frequently bearing the names of the localities.

In distant Babylonia, the exiles of the various villages and towns were drawn together and came to imagine themselves as families and clans.

This is not to deny that there is some evidence that some of the clans and families had been kinship groups before the Exile. As in later times, so in earlier ones, priestly clans and families tended to centre about a particular locality. This has been pointed out for the period after the destruction of the Temple by S. Klein in his monograph *Baraita of the Twenty Mishmarot* (see below, p. 129). In earlier times, apparently, the priests of Anathoth claimed descent from Eliathar, whom King Solomon banished from Jerusalem, and compelled to live there (I Kgs. 2.26).

There seem to be references to the families of Pashhur (very noted in pre-Exilic times) and Meremot (apparently a subclan, mentioned in Neh. 10.6; 12.3) on the ostraca, found in the Temple of Arad, in the Negev. The meaning of these ostraca does not yet seem to be entirely clear. But they indicate that the families of at least some priests known to post-biblical generations had already become kinship groups much earlier (see Y. Aharoni in D. Winton Thomas, *Archaeology and the Study of the OT,* p. 396). But this sense of kinship did not necessarily exist in every case before the Exile, when the people of the various regions regarded one another simply as neighbours. This attitude is reflected in Mishna *Ta'anit* 4.2, which must therefore be considered a product of pre-Exilic thought.

B. The Function of the Jerusalemite Priests and Levites

Mishna *Ta'anit* 4.2 asserts that each region had a representative of Jerusalemites consisting of priests and Levites, as well as Israelites. The function of these Jerusalemite priests and Levites has perplexed the commentators on the Mishna and the Talmud.[5] As the Mishna expressly states that the priests and Levites of each region went up to Jerusalem for their term of ministry, no group of priests and Levites from the Holy City was needed to represent it. And, indeed, the passage in *Tosefta* cited above, as well as many other passages in the Talmud, take it for granted that the *ma'amadot* in Jerusalem consisted only of Israelites. But this was clearly not the view of the authors of the Mishna. What then, according to the Mishna, was the function of these Jerusalemite priests and Levites?

The text of the Mishna becomes intelligible only when we realise that the *mishmarot* were geographical areas, into which the country was divided before the Exile. The Mishna assumes that the priests and Levites of some regions would not be able to participate in the national worship at the Temple of Jerusalem. Yet the inhabitants of that region were entitled to have priests and Levites act for them. Therefore, it was arranged that each region should have a representation of priests and Levites in Jerusalem, to serve as agents for those regions unable to supply their own priests and Levites.

This necessity did not exist in post-Exilic times, when the priests and Levites were divided into families, each

NEW LIGHT FROM THE PROPHETS

assigned a definite term of office at the Temple. The situation contemplated in the Mishna was that of the pre-Exilic age, when most of the regions into which the country was divided belonged to the territory of the Northern Kingdom until 721 B.C.E. The priests and Levites of those regions could not come to Jerusalem for their time of service. Indeed, they might not have accepted Jerusalem as the sole Sanctuary. Yet some of the inhabitants of these regions, at least, accepted the teaching of the centralisation of worship in Jerusalem. To enable such people to share in the Temple service, a representation of priests and Levites residing in Jerusalem was appointed to act for them. For the sake of uniformity, representations were established for every region, even those very near Jerusalem.

C. *The Relation of the Daily Sacrifice to the Various Regions*

According to the Mishna under study, the daily sacrifices at the Temple in Jerusalem were not offered on behalf of the whole people. The rule established by "the early Prophets" (or "the Prophets of Jerusalem") associated daily sacrifices with particular regions into which they divided the country. The Mishna does not, indeed, state that each region bore the cost of the sacrifices offered during its term of service. According to II Chronicles 31.3, the cost of the sacrifices was borne by the king himself. This may be an historical fact. In that event, the regions were only nominally responsible for the sacrifice offered on their behalf. Yet the sacrifice was the responsibility of the region, as the Mishna clearly implies.

This concept of the daily sacrifices as not that of the whole community is rejected by *Tosefta;* by the Great Document found in Nehemiah, Chapters 9-10; and by the general Rabbinic tradition.[6] According to these sources, every member of the community made an equal contribution to the Temple treasury to defray the cost of the daily sacrifice. Mishna *Ta'anit* 4.2, which appears to have no knowledge of this system of contributions and which regards the daily sacrifices as being offered on behalf of the various regions in rotation, must be dated before the Great Document in Nehemiah, Chapters 9-10, and probably before the Exile.

D. The Presence of the Donor at the Time of the Sacrifice of his Offering

Mishna *Ta'anit* 4.2 assumes that one making an offering would himself be present at the time of the sacrifice. The Mishna's rhetorical question—"How can one's sacrifice be offered without one's standing over it?"—suggests that at the time of its authors, this principle was taken for granted. But it is found virtually nowhere in the Talmud outside this passage.[7] And yet, had such a regulation existed, it would probably have been included somewhere in Mishna or *Tosefta*. On the contrary, a number of passages assume one may send one's sacrifice to the Temple without appearing personally at the time of its offering. (See below p. 94).

It follows that Mishna *Ta'anit* 4.2 derives from a time when the presence of the donor at the time of sacrifice was required. However, this rule was later modified. Why? Apparently because the centralisation of worship in Jerusalem made it impracticable to demand the physical presence of the donor in the Sanctuary whenever a sacrifice was offered. He might be ill, and yet desire a sin-offering to be sacrificed on his behalf because he was troubled through a sense of guilt. He might have made a vow, which he wished to fulfil, and yet could not come to the Temple to do so.

The expression of the Mishna, itself—"How can a sacrifice be offered without the donor standing by it?"—suggests memories of sacrifices at private sanctuaries; for in the Temple, the donor never stood near the altar at the time of the sacrifice. His place was in the Court of Israel, at a considerable distance from the altar, which was located in the Court of Priests.

We may, therefore, safely assume that the norm of the Mishna was formulated shortly after the provincial sanctuaries had been abolished. The authors considered the daily sacrifices not those of the whole nation, but of particular regions; and they took it for granted that, aside from the priests and Levites, the residents of the region could not be expected to come to Jerusalem.

E. Participation of Provincial Priests and Levites in the Ministry of the Central Temple

The Mishna clearly asserts that the priests and

Levites of each region went up to Jerusalem for their term of service, to participate in the national worship. These priests and Levites, residing in their various localities, had presumably served originally as ministers of local altars, like the priests of Dan, who claimed descent from Moses (Judg. 18.30 ff.). Such participation of the local priests in the central worship was permitted in the Book of Deuteronomy (18.6 ff.); but was forbidden by King Josiah at the time of his Reformation (II Kgs. 23.9). The provincial priests could be given part of the emoluments of the Temple, but could not minister at the altar, according to the decree of King Josiah.

As the Mishna permits the provincial priests to participate in the worship of the Temple, and indeed requires them to do so, we must take it that it was formulated before the Reformation under Josiah. Its authors were Prophets who flourished during the long reign of Manasseh and the early days of King Josiah. They still adhered (as shown above p. 55) to the common view requiring a donor of a sacrifice to stand by the altar at the time of the ritual. They also believed that the national daily sacrifice could be offered by a region on behalf of the whole nation. And finally, they held with King Hezekiah and his contemporary Prophets that, with the abolition of the local sanctuaries, provision should be made for their priests to participate in the worship at the central Sanctuary.

F. The Relation of the Mishna to the Book of Chronicles, to the Documents in Ezra and Nehemiah, and to the Corresponding Passage in Tosefta

The early date of the passage in the Mishna is further attested by its relation to the Book of Chronicles, which it flatly contradicts. According to I Chronicles 24.3 ff., the priestly courses (families) were fixed by King David and the priests: Zadok for the Eleazar clans, and Ahimelech for the Ithamar clans. The order in which the various courses were to minister was determined by lot (*ibid*. vv. 7 ff.). The division of Levitical clans was made by David and Samuel the Seer (I Chron. 9.22). Nothing is said in the Book of Chronicles about the geographical division of the country, postulated in Mishna *Ta'anit* 4.2. However, the account in the Book of Chronicles involves inherent difficulties as well as inconsistency with Mishna *Ta'anit* 4.2.

Samuel died before David became king (I Sam. 25.1; 28.3). One can hardly envisage David establishing the Levitical courses while still a hunted outlaw. How then could he and the Prophet Samuel have cooperated in the establishment of the Levitical courses? Moreover, according to Mishna *Ta'anit*, quoted above, the twenty-four *mishmarot* of the priests *and the Levites* were established not by King David and his associates, but by the early Prophets. And they were not genealogical groups, but areas of the country.

According to *Tosefta Ta'anit* 2.1 (ed. Lieberman p. 128), the division and order of the priestly clans were fixed in the time of the Second Commonwealth, through a lottery. If the system had already been established during the First Commonwealth by King David and the eponyms of the clans of Eleazar and Ithamar, the lottery would have been unnecessary. Moreover, it is astonishing to find that the order of the priestly clans in all subsequent literature agrees with that of the Book of Chronicles.[8] Presumably, it also followed the division set up through the lottery in the early days of the Second Commonwealth. But only through a miracle could the lottery have determined the order precisely as it had been made centuries earlier by King David. Finally, if each of the families mentioned in Chronicles returned after the Exile, why do Mishna *Ta'anit* and various passages in Ezra and Nehemiah assert that only four came back?

The inconsistency of the account of the origin of the *mishmarot* in the Mishna and *Tosefta* with the Book of Chronicles implies that the former were composed before the latter, or at any rate before its acceptance as a sacred work. Once the Book of Chronicles had been incorporated into the Canon, no tradition opposing it could have been formulated as authoritative. Therefore, the question inevitably arises: Why did the Chronicler reject the Mishnaic record?

A suggestion which readily comes to mind is that the Chronicler interpreted the words "the early Prophets" in the Mishna to mean "the earliest Prophets."[9] The Chronicler considered David not only a king but also a Prophet, a view shared by the homilist of *Sifre* Deuteronomy 1 (p. 2, l. 11).[10]

He probably also included Zadok and Ahimelech among "the earliest Prophets." In this view, he agreed with other early authorities, who considered the chief priests gifted with Prophecy.[11] Indeed, as far as the Chronicler was concerned, the early Levites who composed the Psalms "prophesied" (I Chron. 25.1,2,3).

The geographical division suggested in the Mishna was, as the Chronicler understood it, identical with genealogical lines; for the Chronicler held that each family, subclan, and clan, as well as each tribe, inherited land which Joshua had given its ancestors (Cf. I Chron. 4.22 ff.; 5.8 ff., 11 ff., 23 ff.; 6.39 ff., 57 ff., 65 ff.; 722 ff.; 9.2 ff.; *et al.*).

Because the Chronicler knew of the banishment to Anathoth of Abiathar, descendant of Eli, the priest of Shiloh, by King Solomon (I Kgs. 2.26); and because he traced Abiathar's line to Ithamar, the son of Aaron (I Chron. 24.3), he could not impute the division of the priestly clans, including those deriving from Ithamar, to King Solomon or any successor. Moreover, one of the aims of the Chronicler was to legitimatize the descendants of Ithamar as priests authorized to minister in the Temple. Therefore, he ascribed their recognition to King David, Zadok, and Ahimelech. In this he took issue with Ezekiel who held that the priests of the future Temple would be drawn only from the family of Zadok (Ezek. 44.15 ff.). The manner in which the twenty-four families of the priests and their order of services in the restored Temple of the Second Commonwealth were established is described clearly in *Tosefta Ta'anit* 2.1 (ed. Lieberman p. 128).

According to that passage in *Tosefta,* "Four [priestly] clans [*mishmarot*] came up from the Exile. They were Jedaiah, Harim, Pashhur, and Immer. *The Prophets in Jerusalem* arose and divided them into twenty-four watches. They mixed up [cards bearing their names] and put them into a box. The clan of Jedaiah came and took five, making six with itself. The clan of Harim came and took five, making six with itself. The clan of Pashhur came and took five, making six with itself. The clan of Immer came and took five, making six with itself. The Prophets made the following agreement with them, 'Even if Jehoiarib should come

58

up from the Exile, *none of you* will lose your place because of it. But it [Jehoiarib] will have to become ancillary to it [*i.e.*, the clan in whose term its priests would minister].' "

Tosefta presents considerable difficulties. According to its final assertion, "The Prophets made the following agreement *with them*." With whom? Obviously with the four clans which had returned. But the account continues, "that if the clan of Jehoiarib should return, none of you will lose *your* place because of it. But it [*i.e.*, Jehoiarib] will be ancillary to [or associated with, or counted as part of] *it*." To what does the second "it" refer? Obviously, once more to one of the four clans with which Jehoiarib would come to terms.

But if the clans had, at that time, already been divided into twenty-four subgroups, each serving for one week in the winter and another in the summer, one of these subdivisions rather than the larger clan would be displaced. Of course, it could be argued that the subdivisions of each clan ministered one after the other; so that each of the four clans returning from Babylonia ministered for six weeks in the summer and six more in the winter. The agreement would then have been that Jehoiarib would not be entitled to take the six weeks of any of the major clans, but would be integrated with one of them. However, as we shall see below (p. 69), in actual fact Jehoiarib did ultimately return,[12] and was integrated with one of the subdivisions of Jedaiah.

It seems strange at first sight that the agreement with regard to the clan of Jehoiarib would be ascribed to "Prophets" or "the Prophets," whereas the division of the clans was made by "the Prophets of Jerusalem." Yet this stylistic inconsistency clarifies the record. The use of different terms for the "Prophets" indicates that "the Prophets of Jerusalem," responsible for the division of the clans into twenty-four subdivisions, were not the same as those who made the agreement regarding the clan of Jehoiarib. The two statements probably derive from different records composed at different times. They were combined in the present *baraita* by an editor or transmitter. The Prophets of the Restoration assured the four returning clans of priests that even if, with the increasing prosperity of the new settlement, members of the clan of Jehoiarib, which had refused to be one of the pioneers, should return, their own status would be unaffected. The newcomers would be integrated into one of the clans which had joined Zerubabel in the original return.

In a later generation, with Jerusalem once more a town rather than a hamlet, its Prophets divided the four clans into twenty-four subdivisions, each serving for one week in the winter and another in the summer. By that time members of the clan of Jehoiarib had in fact returned, and were integrated into the clan of Jedaiah.

The statement in *Tosefta* that each of the four clans drew five cards, making six with itself, seems unnecessarily prolix. If the clan of Jedaiah was entitled to six weeks for its six subdivisions, why does *Tosefta* not state simply that it drew six cards, indicating the order in which its subdivisions were to serve? Moreover, if each of the clans which returned with Zerubabel was given six places for its subdivisions, how did it happen that the clan names, Jedaiah, Immer, and Harim, appear also as those of subdivisions with the others (see below, p. 101)? *Tosefta* must mean that while the original clans were divided into groups, each with its own week, one subdivision of each clan retained the name of the clan itself. The subdivision bearing the name of the clan presumably was its most distinguished and influential family. Thus it came about that in the order of the priestly courses, as we shall see, at least two families bearing the names of the returning clans, Jedaiah and Harim, had particularly advantageous terms of ministry.

On this assumption, not only does the passage in *Tosefta* become intelligible, but so do various records in Ezra, Nehemiah, and Chronicles regarding the priestly clans. Like *Tosefta Taʻanit* 2.1, Ezra 2.36 ff., and Nehemiah 7.39 ff, assert that only four priestly clans returned from the Exile with Zerubabel. Their names are identical with those mentioned in *Tosefta*. However, whereas the order in *Tosefta* is Jedaiah, Harim, Pashhur, Immer, that in Ezra 2.36 ff. and Nehemiah 7.39 ff., is Jedaiah, Immer, Pashhur, Harim. The same four major clans reappear in Ezra (10.18 ff.), telling how some priests had married heathen women in the time of Ezra, eighty years after the Restoration.

Four priestly clans are recorded as having had among them members who had taken heathen women to wife. They were the descendants of Jeshua, son of Jozadak, the first High Priest of the Restoration, whose family, as we have observed, belonged to the clan of Jedaiah; and priests of the clans of Immer, Harim, and Pashhur, mentioned in that order. This order differs both from that of *Tosefta* and from that of Ezra 2.36 ff., and Nehemiah 7.39 ff. Perhaps the order followed the number of priests involved in the scandal.

The order of the priestly clans in *Tosefta* coincides, however, with that found in Nehemiah 11.10 ff., and I Chronicles 9.10 ff., where priests, who volunteered to make their homes in Jerusalem, are enumerated. According to the document in these Books, the order of the clans was Jedaiah, Pashhur, Immer. (Harim is unmentioned in that record, perhaps because its members declined to settle in Jerusalem, or because its name was omitted by a copyist. However, it is possible that at one time Pashhur (which was renamed Malkiah, as indicated below, p. 103) actually followed immediately on Jedaiah in the order of the ministries. This tradition, although superseded by other arrangements, seems to have been known as late as the second century, C.E.; see below, p. 66).

The name of Jehoiarib occurs for the first time (chronologically) in this document. In Nehemiah, Jedaiah is described as the son of Jehoiarib; in Chronicles, Jedaiah and Jehoiarib are mentioned as separate families. By the time of Nehemiah, members of the clan of Jehoiarib had obviously returned, as the contemporaries of Zerubabel had anticipated. But in accordance with the agreement of the Prophets of the Restoration, the clan of Jehoiarib was integrated with that of Jedaiah. From that time on, the clans of Jehoiarib and Jedaiah always occurred together, Jehoiarib usually being named first.[13]

Evidently the record in *Tosefta*, according to which the four clans returning with Zerubabel agreed with the Prophets to make Jehoiarib ancillary to one of them should any of its members return subsequently, antedated that in Nehemiah which assumed that Jehoiarib had already returned.

The passage in *Tosefta* even more obviously antedates

the time of Ezra, for the authors of the passage in *Tosefta* take no account of the priests who returned with him, claiming descent from Phineas and from Ithamar (Ez. 8.2). Surely, had the passage in *Tosefta* been composed after Ezra's time, it would have made provision for these newcomers. The document in *Tosefta* antedates by a very long time the Chronicler, according to whom the twenty-four priestly clans enumerated by him and known to all later records (I Chron. 24.7 ff.), were established by King David himself. Had the authors of the statement in *Tosefta* been acquainted with this account in Chronicles, they could scarcely have mentioned the clan of Jehoiarib alone as a possible future addition to the restored priests; they would not have had to discuss also the other nineteen families.

The division of the priests into the twenty-four groups was thus made by "the Prophets of Jerusalem," as *Tosefta Ta'anit* indicates. Presumably this happened during the time of Nehemiah, who established Jerusalem as a city. Perhaps Nehemiah, as Ezekiel Kaufmann maintains on the basis of Nehemiah 13.30, was himself one of the men responsible for this division.[14]

Before that time, the four clans already included twenty-two families, as shown in Nehemiah, Chapter 12. These were evidently genealogical family divisions without significance in the order of the service. The division by "the Prophets of Jerusalem" was necessary because the number of priests had increased; and they had scattered over the land. Some order had to be set up for the rotation of the ministries of the different groups.

It has sometimes been maintained that because Jehoiarib is mentioned first among the priestly clans in I Chronicles 24.7 ff., either that passage or the Book of Chronicles itself is of Maccabean origin. The basis for this claim is that the Maccabean priests belonged to the clan of Jehoiarib (I Macc. 2.1), and for that reason it was given precedence over the clan of Jedaiah, mentioned before it in Nehemiah 11.10, and particularly in I Chronicles 9.10.[15] However, this argument overlooks the fact that primacy in the order of the ministry was by no means necessarily an advantage. The clans which served during the weeks immediately before and during Passover were the privileged ones. The festivals brought hosts of pilgrims to Jerusalem. Coming to the Temple, they not only fulfilled the obligation to perform the pilgrimage, but they also brought other offerings due to Temple and its priests. There were many priestly emoluments to be divided among the members of the family ministering at the time of the pilgrims' arrival. There were sin-offerings, guilt-offerings, thank-offerings, peace-offerings, sacrifices by women who had given birth during the year but who had not come to the Temple until the Passover, and sacrifices offered as part of the ritual of purification from various types of defilement. There were also monetary emoluments of various sorts given the ministering priests of the festival season (*cf. e.g.*, Mishna *Baba Qamma* 9.12, and Mishna *Sukkah* 5.7).

As Mishna *Tamid* 5.1 and particularly *Tosefta Sukkah* 4.24, 25 (ed. Lieberman p. 277) indicate, and as is implied in II Chronicles 23.4,8, ministries always began and ended on the Sabbath day. The outgoing group offered the morning sacrifice and the additional Sabbath offerings. The incoming group offered the afternoon sacrifice and took charge of the placing of the new shewbread in the Temple.

As will be shown below (p. 107), for many generations the order of the ministries began with the first full week of Nisan. Thus, if the first day of Nisan were on a Sabbath, the family of Jehoiarib would begin its services on that afternoon. If the first day of Nisan were on a weekday, Jehoiarib would begin its service on the following Sabbath afternoon. For that reason Jehoiarib is listed by the Chronicler as the first of all the priestly clans. Similarly, all the post-Talmudic compositions listing the priestly clans begin with Jehoiarib. And, while as we have seen (p. 57), in the Qumran calendar Maoziah is listed first, the clan of Jehoiarib is assigned the first full week in Nisan and in Tishri. Following Jehoiarib was always Jedaiah, whose term began on the second Sabbath of Nisan. This might occur on the eighth, ninth, tenth, eleventh, twelfth, thirteenth, or fourteenth day of Nisan, depending on the day of the week with which the month began.

Almost always the family ministering during the week

63

beginning with the first Sabbath of Nisan (Nisan 1-8, or 2-9, or 3-10, or 4-11, or 5-12, or 6-13), namely Jehoiarib, was at a disadvantage in comparison with the family following it. The Jehoiarib priests, who had come to Jerusalem for their semi-annual week of Temple service, were displaced on the Sabbath preceding Passover by the incoming Jedaiah priests. During the days separating the Sabbath marking the end of their week of ministry and the Passover, the Jehoiarib priests had no place in the Temple. They could not participate in the worship, enjoy any of the priestly emoluments, or even remain in the precincts of the Sanctuary. They had to find food and lodging elsewhere in Jerusalem. Being priests, required to maintain the laws of purity and to be particularly careful to avoid defilement just before Passover, their housing problem during this period must have been acute. Yet they could not go home because they would be needed during the Passover festival; and they would then have ample opportunity to enjoy the emoluments available to all priests at that time. Perhaps if the Passover were four or five days off, priests dwelling in the vicinity of Jerusalem might go home for the period between the time of their service and the festival. But those living at a distance had to find homes for themselves and to provide for their food in Jerusalem, crowded as it usually was when the festival drew near.

At some period during the Second Commonwealth, it was probably customary for the family serving during the first week of Nisan to return for the first week of Tishri,[16] with the other families following in the prescribed order. Under such an arrangement, the family of Jehoiarib would find its problems of Nisan recurring in the autumn. Having ministered at the Temple until the eighth, ninth, tenth, or eleventh day of Tishri, they would be left without work, board, or lodging until the Sukkot festival on the fifteenth of the month. On the other hand, the family whose term of office included part or all of the Passover week (*i.e.*, the Jedaiah priests) was in charge of all the sacrifices brought during the festival as free-will offerings. The hides of all whole-burnt offerings brought as voluntary sacrifices belonged to them. They received the first-born animals brought to the Temple for sacrifice, and consequently were given the portions of those animals assigned to the priests. They also received the tithes of animals which the pilgrims brought,[17] and doubtless they received such monies as were due the priests at the time under the norm of *Baba Qamma* (*loc. cit.*). They were likely to receive the various gifts enumerated above, which were brought by pilgrims arriving just in time for the Passover festival.

Thus, the most advantageous ministry of all was that immediately preceding Passover and including part of it. This term was given in the Book of Chronicles and according to all subsequent tradition to the clan of Jedaiah, to which the first High Priest of the Restoration belonged. The clan of Jehoiarib, integrated into that of Jedaiah but made ancillary to it, was given the less desirable term, *viz.* immediately preceding that of Jedaiah. Harim, which as we have seen was always fourth in the order of clans returning with Zerubabel, held the third place in the order of ministry at the Temple, according to the Book of Chronicles and later tradition. Its term of ministry followed immediately upon the Passover (and possibly, the Sukkot) festivals. While this term was less desirable than that of Jedaiah, the clan of Harim had an advantage over all other groups in that it could combine its visit to Jerusalem for the term of its ministry with that for the festival pilgrimage.

The clan of Pashhur, renamed Malkiah,[18] followed Seorim,[19] which followed Harim. Thus, if the first of Nisan occurred on a Sabbath, the clan of Jehoiarib ministered during the week of Nisan 1-8; that of Jedaiah ministered during Nisan 8-14; Harim ministered during the Passover week, Nisan 14-21; and Seorim ministered during Nisan 21-28. Apparently, advantage accrued neither to the family of Malkiah nor to that of Immer, whose term of ministry occurred at the end of Tammuz. The fact that the most advantageous term of the year was assigned to Jedaiah, with Jehoiarib given a less satisfactory term, confirms the record of *Tosefta* according to which Jehoiarib, when its members returned, was made part of Jedaiah, but inferior to its main family.

Memories of the early arrangements by which the four

clans, which returned with Zerubabel, ministered in rotation, seem to underlie the assertion of Ben Zoma in *Sifre Zutta* which, omitted in the first draft of this work, I can now include, because of the appearance of Prof. Saul Lieberman's magnificent study, "*Sifre Zutta*." Num. 28.3, p. 323, reads: "This is the offering made by fire which ye shall bring unto the Lord: he-lambs of the first year, without blemish, *two, day by day*." The words translated, "two, day by day" represent a Hebrew phrase which may be explained by mean, "two for the day." From this *Sifre Zutta* derives the principle that "The lambs must be set aside for the particular day [on which they are to be sacrificed]." Ben Zoma went further. He maintained that each lamb had to be set aside not only for the day when it is to be sacrificed, but with the intent that a particular clan sacrifice it. As on the Sabbath one priestly clan ministered in the morning, and another in the afternoon, the morning lamb had to be set aside for the first and the afternoon lamb for the second group of priests. In the usual Rabbinic fashion, Ben Zoma expressed this idea through mention of specific clans. He said: "The morning sacrifice should [be set aside] for Jedaiah; the afternoon sacrifice for Malkiah."

The rule set down by Ben Zoma assumed that the clan Malkiah followed immediately on that of Jedaiah, a notion contrary to all the traditions regarding the order of the priestly families, described above, p. 57.

However, in view of the fact that Malkiah is probably to be identified with Pashhur (as noted above, p. 64), Ben Zoma's comment, made after the destruction of the Temple, seems to hark back to the earliest period of the Second Temple. Whether Ben Zoma was simply quoting an ancient tradition, which had been superseded through the subdivision of the four clans into twenty-four families, or was suggesting the re-introduction of the ancient system, because he felt an antipathy to the Hasmoneans, and therefore to the clan of Jehoiarib, (which always was mentioned first among the clans in Rabbinic and post-Rabbinic writings), must remain uncertain. But it seems clear that in the system which he either recalled or proposed, Jedaiah was to be the first of the clans, and Malkiah the second; for he would naturally select the first two clans to explain his idea. Usually the Talmud mentions Jehoiarib and Jedaiah in such situations (cf., *e.g.* Mishna *Baba Qamma* 9.12). Ben Zoma's selection of Jedaiah and Malkiah indicate that in the system he had in mind they were the first clans.

In Talmudic times, the place of Malkiah in the system of rotation of clans was weeks after that of Jedaiah. However, it may well be that in early times, Pashhur (re-named Malkiah) followed immediately on Jedaiah.

Thus according to the dictum of Ben Zoma, the lambs set aside for the daily sacrifices on the Sabbath must be differentiated from the beginning. The one for the morning had to be designated for the clan ministering in the morning; that for the afternoon had to be designated for the clan serving at that time. (For further discussion of this passage, and a brilliant explanation of the difficulties involved, see Prof. Saul Lieberman, *Sifre Zutta*, New York 1968, p. 117, and 148).

Tosefta Ta'anit 2.1 (ed. Lieberman p. 328), informs us (as already noted, p. 57) that each of the four priestly clans returning with Zerubabel was assigned six weeks for the Temple Ministry. But *Tosefta* states that each clan picked five cards out of the box, through which the order of the ministry of its constituent families was to be determined. The place of the main family of the clan, the one which, (as already observed), bore the clan name, was not decided by the lottery. Its place had apparently been determined through earlier arrangements; namely, those already indicated. Jedaiah obtained the most advantageous week, not because a card indicated that was its place, but because of its insistence on its prerogative. Jehoiarib was given the second place as ancillary to Jedaiah. Harim was given an almost equally desirable place, because of its strength and influence.

As already noted, (p. 56) the Book of Chronicles (I Chron. 24.7 ff.), maintains that the order of the priestly ministries in the Second Commonwealth (as in the First), was that set by King David and his associates. But in view of the record of *Tosefta*, holding that the order was the result of a lottery, it is hard to understand how it came about that the results of the lottery were identical with those which had been determined centuries earlier by King David. Moreover, why should a lottery be needed if the order of ministries had been fixed by King David himself? It seems patent that the Chronicler simply projected onto the time of King David the system of rotation of priestly families customary in his own time.

Taken together, the records of Mishna *Ta'anit* 4.2 and *Tosefta Ta'anit* 2.1 thus offer a coherent, intelligible account of the origin of the twenty-four priestly clans known in the Second Commonwealth, as well as of the system of *mishmarot* and *ma'amadot*. "The early Prophets" at a certain time (to be determined below, p. 70) divided the country into twenty-four regions. Each region was represented in Jerusalem by a *ma'amad* consisting of priests, Levites, and Israelites resident in the Holy City. The Israelite members of the *ma'amad* were always needed because most people could not come to Jerusalem for a week. The priests and Levites of the *ma'amad* were needed because some regions could supply few, if any, priests and Levites of their own for the Temple ministry. According to the Mishna, the Israelites remaining at home participated in a special form of worship, that of studying and reciting specific passages of the Pentateuch.

A curious passage in *Sifre* Deuteronomy 88 (p. 150) may refer to these two forms of worship: one at the Temple, the other in reading the Torah. Deuteronomy 13.5 commands: "After the Lord your God shall ye walk, and Him shall ye fear, and His commandments shall ye keep, and unto His voice shall ye hearken, and Him shall ye serve, and unto Him shall ye cleave." The phrase, "And Him shall ye serve," is explained in *Sifre* as follows: "Worship Him in His Torah; worship Him in His Temple." The identification of study as an act of worship is of course found elsewhere (cf., *e.g., Sifre* Deut. 41, p. 87). However, the passage in *Sifre* Deuteronomy 88 seems to have special significance, because it equates worship through study of Torah with that of the Temple; and even mentions study of Torah before worship in the Temple.

On the assumption that Mishna *Ta'anit* 4.2 records an historical fact, the question arises: Did "the early Prophets" establish regions only for the Southern Kingdom, or for the whole land of Israel? The Mishna does not answer the question; it simply asserts that the Prophets created twenty-four *mishmarot*. However, the assumption that these *mishmarot* covered the whole country seems necessary in order to explain the record in *Tosefta Ta'anit* 2.1.

If the whole land of Israel consisted of twenty-four *mishmarot*, we would expect only four or five of them to have been located in Judah, which contained only two whole tribes and a fragment of a third (*i.e.*, Judah itself, Benjamin, and the disappearing tribe of Simeon) out of a total of twelve land-owning tribes. Thus, we would expect to find people from only four or five *mishmarot* among the deportees to Babylonia. Naturally the priests of each region who had worshipped together in Jerusalem came to regard one another as kinsmen.

The priestly clans in Babylonia therefore, were Jedaiah, Immer, Pashhur, Harim, and Jehoiarib. Members of the first four returned with Zerubabel; but those of Jehoiarib came later. Following the precedent established in the First Commonwealth, the Prophets of Jerusalem at some period following the Restoration (perhaps in the time of Nehemiah) divided the four groups of returning priests into twenty-four *mishmarot*, each of which served at the Temple one week in the winter and another in the summer. But the word *mishmarot* now had a new significance. The four clans which returned from the Exile were called *mishmarot* because originally each had come from a specific *mishmar*. Ultimately the term came to be applied to each of the twenty-four families into which the priesthood was divided and each of which served for two weeks at the Temple. When members of the Jehoiarib clan arrived in Jerusalem, they were integrated, as originally agreed, with one of the subclans of Jedaiah; that is, the one serving at the beginning of the Temple year.

But when was Mishna *Ta'anit* 4.2 composed? And when was the system of *mishmarot* and *ma'amadot* which it describes, established? The fact that the authors of the Mishna regarded the groups of ministering priests and Levites not as kinsmen but as neighbours indicates (as already remarked p. 50), that it was composed before the Restoration, for in all the works deriving from the time of the Restoration onward, the various groups of priests descended from ancestors living in the same locality were considered kinsmen. They could not have been contemporaries of King David and King Solomon, for the system of regions was necessitated only through the centralization of the sacrificial worship in Jerusalem. And passage after passage in the Book of Kings shows that worship at local altars existed until the time of Hezekiah.

On the other hand, "the early Prophets" could not have been contemporaries of King Josiah, acting in the wake of his Reformation. We are specifically told that as a result of that Reformation, the priests of the local altars were denied the right to participate in the worship at Jerusalem (II Kgs. 23.9), whereas Mishna *Ta'anit* 4.2 gave provincial priests that right.

"The early Prophets" under consideration were therefore, in all probability, contemporaries of King Hezekiah. This would seem to be implied by the nature of the institutions established by them, and the political and administrative context calling for these institutions. King Hezekiah had suppressed the provincial altars, as the ambassadors of Sennacherib charged (II Kgs. 18.22). Having done so, he also bestowed on the provincial priests the right to worship in Jerusalem. The Prophets, associated with him in this centralization of worship, divided the whole land of Israel into twenty-four *mishmarot* or regions.

This was done despite the fact that Hezekiah was king of only a small part of the land; namely, of the little kingdom of Judah; for with the collapse of the Northern Kingdom, Hezekiah naturally hoped that at some time its territory would be reunited with that of Judah under the dynasty of King David. In this hope he was supported by the Prophets of Jerusalem; for the Prophets had never recognized as permanent the division of Israel into two kingdoms. While waiting for the political re-unification of the land, King Hezekiah and the contemporary Prophets sought to win the remaining inhabitants of the former Northern Kingdom to the religion of their ancestors. One way was to create loyalties to the Sanctuary in Jerusalem. The system of *mishmarot* and *ma'amadot* was an excellent device to accomplish this purpose.

Every Israelite would be directly associated with the system of worship at the Temple in Jerusalem. The local priests and Levites would minister at that Temple two weeks a year, and the rest of the people would assemble locally during those two weeks for nonsacrificial worship: the reading of the Torah.

The residents of the former Northern Kingdom were represented in Jerusalem by priests and Levites who lived in that city. For the sake of uniformity, similar groups of priests and Levites were created also for the Judaite regions, although the priests and Levites of those regions came to Jerusalem for their period of service. If the priests and Levites of the Southern Kingdom came from five regions and thus consisted of five groups, each might well come to consider itself a clan during the Exile. Thus, the Judaite exiles in Babylonia would have included five clans of priests deriving from the Southern Kingdom, *i.e.,* Judah.

Hence, at the end of the Exile there were five recognized clans of priests of the Temple in Jerusalem. Members of all but one returned with Zerubabel. In time, when Jerusalem had become more than a hamlet and many Israelites had settled in remote villages, it became necessary to provide for regular service at the Temple. Adopting the principle of rotation established in pre-Exilic times, "the Prophets of Jerusalem" (as *Tosefta Ta'anit* 2.1 records) divided the four clans which had come with Zerubabel into twenty-four sub-clans, each charged with ministry at the Temple for one week in the winter and another in the summer. The restored clans doubtless included some priests who traced their descent to Eli and his family, who had ministered at Shiloh and had been ousted by King Solomon. Their legitimacy as priests in Jerusalem may have been under attack from the Zadokites. Hence the effort of the Chronicler to establish their legitimacy by tracing their authorization to King David and the Prophet Samuel. *Tosefta Ta'anit* 3(4),2 goes further, maintaining that their legitimacy was established by Moses himself.

The Chronicler, like *Tosefta Ta'anit* 3(4).2 calls Samuel "the Seer" (I Chron. 26.28). While the Book of Samuel (I Sam. 9.9) specifically states that in early times a Prophet was called "a Seer," the use of that term in Chronicles seems strange. Perhaps this identification of Samuel as a Seer rather than a Prophet was in some way associated with the distinction between him and the later Prophets drawn in the early document underlying the opening Mishna of *Abot* (see below, p. 79).

The assertion of *Tosefta Ta'anit* 2.1 that the arrangement was made by "the Prophets of Jerusalem" offers further support for the hypothesis here developed. Normally one would suppose that such an arrangement would be made by the Temple priests. In fact it was they who, according to I Chronicles 24.6, took the leading part in the establishment of the twenty-four priestly clans. One would expect them to play this role again in the division of the priesthood after the Restoration. Why did this responsibility fall on "the Prophets of Jerusalem?" Apparently the reason that this responsibility was imposed on "the Prophets of Jerusalem" in the time of Nehemiah, was that it was known that "the early Prophets," who had invented the institution of the twenty-four regions, each with its own representation in Jerusalem, were Prophets dwelling in Jerusalem. It was doubtless at their urging that Hezekiah had suppressed the provincial altars; and at their urging he agreed to permit the provincial priests to participate in the Temple ministry. The authority of "the Prophets of Jerusalem" in the time of Ezra and Nehemiah was therefore based on the precedent established in the time of Hezekiah. Perhaps, indeed, the original text of the Mishna, telling of the establishment of the *mishmarot* before the Exile, read "the Prophets of Jerusalem," as the corresponding passage in *Tosefta* 3(4).2. (ed. Lieberman p. 337) still has it.

The origin of the priestly *mishmarot* as divisions of the country in pre-Exilic times explains an enigma with regard to the whole system followed during the Second Commonwealth. Why were there twenty-four *mishmarot*? Rotation of the priestly groups, each ministering one week in the winter and one in the summer, was based on the lunar year which normally consists of fifty weeks plus four or five days. Therefore, one would expect the Temple priests to be divided into twenty-five groups. While it is true that all the priests were expected to be at the Temple during the festival weeks, the cycle of the priestly rotation was not interrupted by that fact; for the *mishmar* responsible for the ministry during the festival week remained in charge of all sacrifices not connected with the holiday.[20] At one time (as noted below, p. 105), a system was introduced according to which the priestly clans rotated without interruption and with no regard for the calendar. But this institution probably did not apply (as shown below, p. 110) until the very last years of the Second Temple. However, if the *mishmarot* were originally regions of the country, each responsible for the sacrificial service at the Temple during one week in the summer and another in the winter, no arrangement was needed for the festival weeks. At that time, the whole people was expected to be at the Sanctuary. And so were all the priests and all the Levites. Consequently, only twenty-four regions were needed.

After the Restoration when the ministry at the Temple was divided among the priestly clans, as they were then known, the traditional division into twenty-four was retained. However, with the concept that daily sacrifices were all given on behalf of all Israel, the system of rotation came to be considered only as relating to the priestly and Levitical clans. Therefore, the regular daily sacrifices, and similar offerings not connected with the festivals, were placed in the charge of a particular family ministering at the time. Perhaps one reason for this development was the great advantage which accrued, (as we have seen above, p. 63) to the clan ministering during the festival week. It was also easier to divide the four major clans into twenty-four than into twenty-five families.

It is significant that the norm of the Mishna permitting the former provincial priests to function in Jerusalem was not observed during the Reformation under King Josiah. On the contrary, as already noted, Josiah forbade the priests of the "high places," which he suppressed, to minister in Jerusalem (II Kgs. 23.9), permitting them only limited perquisites of the priesthood "among their brethren." It is significant, too, that the commission sent by the king to inquire of the Prophets what should be done after the discovery of the Scroll of the Torah in the Temple, consulted not Jeremiah but the Prophetess Huldah (II Kgs. 22.14). The

Book of Kings remarks that she was dwelling in Jerusalem, in the new city, and apparently her husband was associated with the government itself. We may perhaps assume that although she belonged to the Prophetic group, opposing the idolatries practiced under Manasseh and desiring to see the worship centralized in Jerusalem, she did not know the tradition preserved in the Prophetic schools which protected the rights of the rural priests.

The early origin of the system of *mishmarot* and *ma'amadot* explains another enigma hitherto puzzling; namely, why the members of the *ma'amad* did not participate in the usual service of the synagogue and, according to some passages, did not even don the *tephillin*. In the Mishna describing the worship of the *ma'amadot,* no mention is made of the usual public prayers or the reading of the weekly portions of the Pentateuch on Mondays and Thursdays. According to Mishna *Megillah* 3.4, in Rabbinic times the regular cycle of weekly readings from the Torah was interrupted for the various festivals and also for the *ma'amadot.* But why? Would it not have been natural to read the regular portion of the week, together with the assigned section of Genesis?

Mishna *Ta'anit* states that during the *ma'amadot* the priestly blessing was recited four times: "in the morning service, at *musaf,* in the afternoon service, and at the closing of the gates." *Tosefta Ta'anit* 3(4).1, (ed. Lieberman p. 336), however, substitutes for the word *musaf,* "midday." Commentators accepting the text of the Mishna have had some difficulty in explaining the word *musaf* there, because there is no *musaf* service on fast days and at the *ma'amadot.* The *musaf* service, replacing the additional sacrifices of Sabbaths, new moons, and festivals, is said on no other days. The commentators have therefore postulated the existence of some special prayer recited at midday during the *ma'amadot,* although none is mentioned in the Talmudic sources.

But the difficulty involves more than the *ma'amadot.* It is clear from evidence found throughout the Talmud that *musaf* prayer of Sabbaths and festivals was unknown before the destruction of the Temple;[21] and indeed was invented after its destruction in reminiscence of the additional sacrifices of those days. It is even unlikely that there was any afternoon service in the synagogue before the destruction of the Temple, and surely there was none at the "closing of the gates" of the Temple.

The Mishna dealing with *ma'amadot* describes conditions prevailing during the existence of the Temple; for after its destruction the whole system of *ma'amadot* ceased. The Mishnaic norm composed during Temple times could not have made mention of a *musaf* prayer service. We must therefore accept as original the reading "midday" found in *Tosefta*. The Mishnaic norm enumerated not synagogue services but times of the day. *Shaharit* in this passage did not mean the early morning prayer, but dawn. The second period for the priestly blessing was midday, as *Tosefta* states. The third was the afternoon,[22] the fourth the time of the closing of the Temple gates. However, the Mishna, speaking of these periods, applies equally to the *ma'amadot,* the fast days, and the Day of Atonement. Its words must have the same meaning in all three connections. This leads to the conclusion that the Mishna did not yet know of regular prayer services on the Day of Atonement, or at any rate did not associate the priestly blessing (now a standard part of the *'amidah*) with the prayer services.

This conclusion implies that the Mishna (in its original form) was composed in very early times; for, surely, the priestly benediction was added to the synagogue prayer service no later than the time of the persecutions of Antiochus. But the Mishna must be even earlier than this suggestion indicates: for if there had been regular synagogue services at the time of its composition, they could not have been ignored in the discussion of the ritual of the priestly blessings. We are therefore led to conclude that the Mishna was composed before there were regular synagogue services, such as came to be known in later times. This would indicate that the Mishna derives at the earliest from the fifth or fourth century B.C.E.[23]

The discussion above points, of course, to a much earlier date for the origin of the *ma'amadot*. The early date of the passage in the Mishna, associated with the *ma'amadot,* underscores the likelihood that the institution itself was of pre-Exilic origin. This argument is unaffected by the tradition transmitted in *Tosefta Ta'anit* 3(4).1, (ed. Lieberman p. 336) according to which the priestly blessing was pronounced only in the morning. Doubtless, the difference between the two traditions developed either because in the course of time the priestly blessing at the afternoon service was omitted, or because various regions had different customs in this regard. But the norm, transmitted in the name of R. Meir, apparently was that of the Temple priests themselves, and was formulated no later then the fifth or fourth century B.C.E.

CHAPTER X

THE PRE-EXILIC ORIGIN OF
MISHNA *ABOT* 1.1

In this chapter, it will be demonstrated that the opening section of Mishna *Abot,* now greatly revised, was originally composed by pre-Exilic Prophets. Its purpose was to establish the position of the Prophets as interpreters of the Law, as the rightful successors of Moses, as exegetes, scholars, and judicial authorities. The authors of this document, in its original form, rejected the juristic authority of the priests of the Temple of Jerusalem, and probably directed their appeal primarily to the population of northern Israel after its independence had been destroyed by Assyria in 722 B.C.E. The document was therefore the work of prophetic teachers who flourished some time between 722 B.C.E. and the fall of Jerusalem in the year 586 B.C.E. Careful analysis of Mishna *Abot* 1.1, and of the corresponding passages in *Abot of R. Nathan* (ARN) I and II, furnishes the evidence for this early date of the original composition.

Mishna *Abot* 1.1 now reads: "Moses received Torah[1] from Sinai, and transmitted it to Joshua; Joshua to the Elders; the Elders to the Prophets; the Prophets to the Men of the Great Synagogue." After citing the maxim of the Men of the Great Synagogue, the Mishna records a saying of Simeon the Righteous, who was "one of the survivors of the Great Synagogue." It then records that "Antigonus of Socho received [the tradition] from Simeon the Righteous," and quotes the maxim of Antigonus.[2] The record of transmission of Torah from Moses to Antigonus of Socho is followed by another, tracing the history through the five "Pairs." These "Pairs" consisted of the heads of the Pharisaic schools between the time of Antigonus and that of Hillel and Shammai, the contemporaries of Herod. In Mishna *Abot,* Chapter I concludes with the maxims of Rabban Gamaliel I, the grandson of Hillel, and Rabban Simeon ben Gamaliel I, each of whom headed the Pharisaic schools in his time.

Thus there were, according to this Mishna, seven links in a chain of tradition leading from Moses to Antigonus of Socho; and seven more leading from Antigonus of Socho to Rabban Simeon ben Gamaliel I, the last head of the Pharisees before the destruction of the Temple by Titus. There were fourteen stages in the transmission of Torah from Moses to Rabban Simeon ben Gamaliel I. We shall see the great significance which, according to these early compilers and transmitters, attached to the numbers seven and fourteen in this context.[3]

The significance of Mishna *Abot* 1.1 is clarified through a study of the corresponding passages of ARN I and II. In ARN I, the chain of tradition is described as follows:

"Joshua received [Torah] from Moses, as it is said, 'And thou shalt put of thy honour on him, that all the congregation of the children of Israel may hearken' (Num. 27.20). The Elders received [it] from Joshua, as it is said, 'And the people served the Lord all the days of Joshua, and all the days of the Elders who outlived Joshua, who had seen the great work of the Lord that he had wrought for Israel' (Judg. 2.7). The Judges received [it] from the Elders, as it is said, 'And it came to pass in the days when the Judges judged' (Ruth 1.1). The Prophets received [it] from the Judges, as it is said, 'And I sent you all my servants and Prophets, sending them daily betimes and often' (Jer. 7.25).

"Haggai, Zechariah, and Malachi received [it] from the Prophets. The Men of the Great Synagogue received [it] from Haggai, Zechariah, and Malachi."

Thus, the seven links in the chain of tradition are: Moses; Joshua; the Elders; the Judges; the Prophets; Haggai, Zechariah, and Malachi; and the Men of the Great Synagogue. When the Mishna underlying ARN I was formulated, Simeon the Righteous and Antigonus of Socho were not yet included among the authoritative exegetes. We must consider the possibility that this was because the document was composed before their time.

In an introduction to its chain of tradition, ARN II

quotes Mishna *Abot* in its present form. It then proceeds to say: "Moses received Torah neither through an angel, nor through a seraph, but from the King of kings of kings, The Holy One, blessed be He, as it is said. . . ." [Here follow verses from Leviticus and Deuteronomy establishing this fact].

ARN II then describes the chain of tradition as follows: "Moses transmitted the Torah to Joshua, as it is said, 'And Joshua, the son of Nun, was full of the spirit of wisdom, for Moses had laid his hands upon him' (Deut. 34.9). Joshua transmitted [it] to the Elders, as it is said, 'And the people served the Lord. . . .' (Judg. 2.7). The Elders transmitted [it] to the Judges, as it is said, 'And when He raised up Judges for them' (Judg. 2.18). *The Judges transmitted [it] to Eli,* as it is said, 'And Eli, the priest, sat upon his seat' (I Sam. 1.9). [The author may have taken the word *kiso* to mean not "seat" or "chair," but "throne," indicating that Eli held a place of great authority.] *Eli transmitted [it] to Samuel,* as it is said, 'And the child Samuel grew before the Lord' (I Sam. 2.21). Samuel transmitted [it] to the Prophets, as it is said, 'For the Lord God will do nothing, except that He revealeth His counsel to His servants the Prophets' (Amos 3.7).

"The Prophets transmitted [it] to Haggai, Zechariah, and Malachi. Haggai, Zechariah, and Malachi transmitted [it] to the Men of the Great Synagogue."

The statement in ARN II concerning Eli and Samuel, omitted in ARN I and in the Mishna, is apparently part of the original text. It could not have been added to ARN II by a late editor. Such an editor would surely have considered Samuel one of the Prophets. He would have had no reason to mention him separately, or to mention Eli, the priest of Shiloh, at all.

We thus arrive at the conclusion that in the parent text of ARN, and therefore in the Mishna *Abot* underlying it, the chain of tradition was as still in ARN II:

Moses	Eli
Joshua	The Prophets
The Elders	Haggai, Zechariah and Malachi
The Judges	The Men of the Great Synagogue
Samuel	

Significantly, both ARN I and II distinguished the Prophets from Haggai, Zechariah, and Malachi, although everywhere else in Rabbinic writings it is assumed that they were Prophets. The authors of both ARN I and II (and therefore of their parent text) do not call the pre-Exilic Prophets "early Prophets," as is usual. On the contrary, they denominate them simply, Prophets.

It is further significant that whereas ARN I and II demonstrate the authority of most individuals and groups in their chains of tradition through reference to biblical verses, neither cites any verse to support the claims of Haggai, Zechariah and Malachi or those of the Men of the Great Synagogue.

It seems obvious from the fact that the pre-Exilic Prophets are called simply "Prophets" rather than "Early Prophets," that the oldest text of Mishna *Abot* knew no post-Exilic Prophets. The names of Haggai, Zechariah, and Malachi and the Men of the Great Synagogue were added by an editor of a later period. He could not find any verses to substantiate the claims of these authorities as transmitters of the tradition. But he did not dare expunge from the record the verses cited in the older text.

It follows that the original document, from which the names of Haggai, Zechariah and Malachi were omitted, was composed either during the Exile or before it.

Presumably, the earliest document dealing with the chain of authority resembled the text of ARN. It not only cited the various links of tradition, but supported the claim of each individual or group with an appropriate biblical verse. The more terse statement in the present Mishna was an abbreviation of the older form, made in order to avoid the clumsiness of mentioning biblical verses in support of the claims of some authorities, and not in for others.

We have noticed that according to Mishna *Abot* 1.1, there were seven links in the chain of tradition from Moses to Antigonus of Socho; and seven more from Jose ben Joezer and Jose ben Zeredah to Rabban Simeon ben Gamaliel I. The number seven played an important part also in the text underlying ARN I and II.

The three versions should be studied side by side to see the importance attaching to the number of links in the chain of tradition.

Mishna *Abot*	ARN I	ARN II
1. Moses	1. Moses	1. Moses
2. Joshua	2. Joshua	2. Joshua
3. The Elders	3. The Elders	3. The Elders
4. The Prophets	4. The Judges	4. The Judges
5. The Men of the Great Synagogue	5. The Prophets	5. Eli
6. Simeon the Righteous	6. Haggai, Zechariah and Malachi	6. Samuel
7. Antigonus of Socho	7. The Men of the Great Synagogue	7. The Prophets
		8. Haggai, Zechariah and Malachi
		9. The Men of the Great Synagogue

As we have observed, (above p. 78), the parent text of ARN I and II did not contain the names of Haggai, Zechariah, and Malachi, having been formulated before their time. In ARN II, the names of those Prophets were added together with the Men of the Great Synagogue, to bring the chain of tradition down to contemporary leaders. The editors of ARN II saw fit to omit the names of Eli and Samuel, so that their list would still contain only seven links. The authors of Mishna *Abot,* likewise respecting the number seven, but desiring to bring the chain of tradition down to the time of Antigonus of Socho, omitted the Judges and included Haggai, Zechariah and Malachi among the Prophets.

At first glance it may appear strange that such emphasis should be put on the fact that the Prophets, or in the later version the Men of the Great Synagogue, constituted the seventh stage in the transmission of Torah. But seven was a sacred number; and it was natural to believe that with the seventh step in its history, the Torah, like many other institutions, would come into a new epoch in its development.[4] After all, one could not forget that Moses and Aaron were the seventh link in the chain of descent from Abraham; that Enoch, the saint among the antediluvian patriarchs, the man who had been physically translated to heaven, was the seventh in the list which began with Adam. That the ancient transmitters considered the number seven especially significant to their argument is apparent from the comment in the opening sections of ARN II. After stressing the fact that Moses was "purified" in the cloud for seven days before he was admitted into the Divine presence to receive Torah, ARN II (chap. I, ed. Schechter 1a) gives a list of other phenomena requiring seven days. ARN II reads: "Hence they said, (the time of purification of) a man afflicted with a flow is seven (days);[5] (that of) a woman with a flow is seven (days);[6] (that of) a menstruating woman is seven (days);[7] that of one defiled through contact with a corpse is seven (days);[8] the time of mourning is seven (days);[9] the time of wedding festivities is seven (days)."[10]

It is true that each of these examples concerns measurable time; but the authors of the Mishna apparently considered their chain of tradition one which also consisted of eras. Only the seventh era was one in which a stable and permanent organization for the transmission of Torah came into being. The several versions of the ancient document differed about what this seventh era was. According to the original document, it was the age of the Prophets; a later editor made it the age of the Men of the Great Synagogue. Still later, the number fourteen was substituted for seven, and it was held that only with the fourteenth stage did the history of transmission of Torah reach its climax in the Schools of Shammai and Hillel.[11] Finally, R. Judah the Patriarch suggested that the ultimate authority was the dynasty of Hillel from which he himself was descended. It is probable that opposing groups maintained that the final stage came with the rise of the Academy of Yabneh under Rabban Johanan ben Zakkai.[12]

The Mishna in all its versions, was a proclamation of the authority of the non-priestly scholars as opposed to that of the Temple priests. It was used by the Pharisaic teachers, spiritual heirs of the Prophets and the Men of the Great Synagogue, to show that they, and not the contemporary High Priests, were the authorized interpreters of the Law, the successors of Moses, Joshua, and the Elders. As an affirmation of the authority of the Pharisaic scholars as exegetes, this document was supremely important to the members of the Pharisaic movement. That is why it became customary to recite it on every Sabbath between Passover and Shabuot.[13] As the text became larger, through the addition of later maxims and compilations of maxims, it was divided into chapters, one chapter being recited every Sabbath afternoon. As there were only five chapters, a sixth had to be added for the sixth Sabbath between Passover and Shabuot. (The custom still survives in an expanded form; one of the Chapters of the Fathers is recited every Sabbath afternoon between Passover and Rosh ha-Shanah.)

It was particularly necessary to recite the document between Passover and Shabuot because the date of Shabuot was the subject of controversy between the Pharisees and the priests.[14] This was a most bitter controversy because it affected the observance of religious ritual by each individual as well as in the Temple itself. The priests could, of course, follow their own doctrine in the Temple, observing Shabuot there according to their own calendar. From the Pharisaic point of view, however, they were not observing the festival at all, and any Judean who accepted the priestly calendar was violating the Law by working on the real feast day, abstaining from work only on an ordinary weekday. The Proto-Pharisaic[15] teachers, as well as the Pharisees themselves, feeling compelled to persuade the people to follow the Pharisaic tradition, had instituted the custom of reciting this part of the Mishna because their claim as authoritative exponents of Torah was contained in it.

It is curious that, to demonstrate the place of the Judges in the chain of tradition, ARN I cites Ruth 1.1 instead of the far more pertinent and convincing passage in Judges 2.18 which is cited in ARN II. The reason for this choice may have been to affirm the sanctity of the Book of Ruth. It follows from this consideration that the original document did, in fact, rely on Judges 2.18.

ARN I and II differ also in regard to the evidence for Joshua's role in the chain of tradition. ARN II cites the Deuteronomic verse affirming Joshua's wisdom. ARN I cites the Divine command in Numbers that Moses bestow some of his glory on Joshua. In this instance, too, the verse cited in ARN II is more convincing than that in ARN I. Perhaps it may be assumed that the verse cited in the parent document underlying both ARN I and II was Deuteronomy 34.9 rather than Numbers 27.20. The citation from Numbers may have been substituted for that from Deuteronomy by a pro-priestly editor, because it is in Numbers that Joshua's authority is subordinated to that of Eleazer the priest. (For the Shammaitic, and therefore pro-priestly, influence in the transmission of this part of ARN I, see JBL LVII, p. 16, and my *Introduction to the Treatise Abot and Abot of R. Nathan,* pp. 17 ff.) Finally, ARN II quotes the verse from Amos in support of the role of the Prophets; ARN I quotes Jeremiah.

But how could the authority of the Prophets be established through a quotation from a Prophet? Why did the authors of the document not base their argument on Deuteronomy 18.18, which promises Israel that they will have Prophets similar to Moses himself? The answer must be that the authors were trying to counter a notion that could mistakenly be derived from Deuteronomy 18.18; *i.e.,* that the Prophets would be capable of playing the role of wizards and magicians, such as were found among other peoples. In this verse, it is in the context of the prohibition of magic that the promise to send Prophets to Israel is given.

There is evidence that the pre-Exilic Prophets claimed juridical authority in the interpretation of the Torah, much of that interpretation apparently went back to the oral traditions of Amos (see above, pp. 22). Because this interpretation was by no means obvious, the authors of the document could not cite the verse from Deuteronomy. They could cite Amos, whose status as a Prophet, in the sense of one possessing judicial authority, was accepted. The verse from Amos supported the view that the Divine counsel, which included the authority to interpret Divine commandments as to righteous action, was revealed to the Prophets. On the other hand, the verse from Jeremiah could not possibly be interpreted as justifying the claim of the Prophets to be inspired jurists. Jeremiah described them only as messengers sent to admonish the people, warning them of impending peril, as he himself did. Thus ARN I rejected the verse declaring the Prophets authorized interpreters of Torah, as it rejected the verse making the same claim for Joshua. Its pro-priestly editors held rather that the priests alone were appropriate interpreters of Torah. The original documents underlying both ARN I and II must have cited Amos.

Another significant difference between the texts of the document in ARN I and II requires explanation. While in ARN I each individual or group in the chain of tradition after Moses is described as having "received" the tradition from an earlier authority, ARN II and the Mishna both describe the same process as one in which the earlier authority "transmitted" the tradition to the later one. It is only after the mention of Simeon the Righteous that the Mishna and ARN II use the word "receive" in reference to the chain of tradition. This reading of the Mishna and ARN II was apparently introduced by R. Akiba or his disciples because the earlier text, speaking of one authority "receiving" Torah from another, might have been interpreted as referring to an Oral Tradition. Indeed, it apparently had that connotation in the description of all the links in the chain of tradition following Simeon the Righteous.

It was the contention of R. Akiba and his School that Moses received the Scroll of the Torah from Mt. Sinai and handed it to Joshua, and that this was the Torah given by Joshua to the Elders, and they to their successors. According to this School, only beginning with Simeon the Righteous does the Mishna record the transmission of the Oral Tradition. Presumably, the term *qibbel* ("he received") was originally employed throughout the document[16] to claim that Joshua "received" oral tradition from Moses, the Elders from Joshua, and so on.[17] But R. Akiba denied the existence of an entity called the "Oral Torah," holding that all the teachings ascribed to the Oral Torah could be deduced by careful study of the Written Pentateuch.[18] In a passage in *Sifra*, R. Akiba rejected not only the view of Rabban

Gamaliel II, which he explicitly controverted, but apparently that of the whole earlier Pharisaic tradition regarding the "Oral Law."

This remarkable view of R. Akiba has not yet received the attention it deserves. It apparently underlies the controversy between R. Johanan and R. Eleazer, found in *B. Gittin* 60b. According to R. Johanan, "Most of the Torah was given orally and only a little in writing." R. Johanan was of this opinion because he held that virtually the whole Jewish tradition consisted of norms found in the Mishna and other collections, transmitted from teacher to pupil. He paid comparatively little attention to the older commentaries on the Pentateuch, apparently believing that the *Midrashim* simply associated transmitted norms with verses. That would seem to be why he did not study until late in life so basic a text as *Sifra*,[19] the commentary on Leviticus. R. Eleazer, who spent much time in mastering that and doubtless similar works, stated that "most of the Torah is that which is written, and only a small part is oral."[20] He held, as R. Akiba had evidently taught, that virtually the whole of the Oral Tradition could be derived by proper exegesis of the Written Pentateuch. Hence there was no need for a separate Oral Tradition.[21]

Therefore, the original Prophetic document underlying ARN I and II, and which became the basis for Mishna *Abot* 1.1 probably read approximately as follows: "Moses was sanctified in the cloud, and received Torah from Sinai. Joshua received [it] from Moses, as it is said, 'And Joshua, the son of Nun, was full of the spirit of wisdom, for Moses had laid his hands upon him.' The Elders received [it] from Joshua, as it is said, 'And the people served the Lord all the days of Joshua, and all the days of the Elders that outlived Joshua, who had seen the great work of the Lord, that He had wrought for Israel.' The Judges received [it] from the Elders, as it is written, 'And when He raised up Judges for them.' Eli received [it] from the Judges, as it is said, 'And Eli, the priest, sat on his throne.' Samuel received [it] from Eli, as it is said, 'And the child Samuel grew. . . .' The Prophets received [it] from Samuel, as it is said, 'For the Lord God will do nothing, except that He revealeth His counsel to His servants, the Prophets.' "

According to the early document, the chain of tradition from Moses to the time of its authors, *viz.* the pre-Exilic or Exilic Prophets, consisted of seven links: Moses, Joshua, the Elders, the Judges, Eli, Samuel, the Prophets. This document was a proclamation defending the authority of the Prophets and, in its changed form, it continued to be used during the Proto-Pharisaic and Pharisaic periods to defend the authority of the lay Sages. It proclaimed the juridical and exegetical authority of the Prophets, as opposed to the priests of the Temple of Jerusalem. Patently, this early document, which traced the transmission of the tradition only to the pre-Exilic Prophets, was used by the author of the passage in *Sifre* Deuteronomy 357 (p. 428), already noted. In this passage *Sifre* comments on the fact that Moses was called "the servant of the Lord" in Deuteronomy 34.5. *Sifre* says: "Scripture does not speak deprecatingly of Moses [in calling him the servant of the Lord], but in his praise; for thus we find that the *early Prophets* were called servants, as it is said, 'For the Lord God will do nothing, but He revealeth it to His servants, the Prophets' (Amos 3.7)."

We may assume, as with other passages in *Sifre* Deuteronomy already discussed, that this one was composed either during the Exile or shortly after the Restoration. The author knew of contemporary Prophets, but he could not know whether the term "servant of the Lord," which he regarded as one of high distinction, would be applied to them. The verse in Amos might describe only pre-Exilic Prophets. What basis did the author have for drawing this distinction between the pre-Exilic Prophets and the later ones? Surely, he inferred it from the document under consideration. In this, as observed above, evidence was adduced to show that the Prophets had received the tradition from Samuel, and through him and his predecessors from Moses. The evidence consisted of the verse from Amos. But the author of the passage in *Sifre* knew that the Prophets to whom the document referred were pre-Exilic. He therefore inferred that Amos meant only pre-Exilic Prophets; and consequently, could say only that the verse showed that "the early Prophets" were called servants.

On the basis of *Sifre* Deuteronomy 357, the author of

a passage in *Sifre* Deuteronomy 27 (p. 43) also asserted that "the early Prophets" were called servants, and demonstrated this fact through the citation of the verse from Amos. The passage in *Sifre* Deuteronomy 27 contains much material of later date than that of *Sifre* Deuteronomy 357, under study. Clearly, it was composed long after the early years of the Restoration, for it cites Ezekiel, Haggai, Job, and Daniel. It therefore identifies the Prophets to whom Amos refers as pre-Exilic, in order to distinguish them from contemporary Prophets. It explains the verse from Amos as it does because of the influence of *Sifre* Deuteronomy 357, the author of which was himself guided by the document underlying Mishna *Abot* 1.1.

To whom was the proclamation underlying Mishna *Abot* 1.1, originally addressed? We have observed that the authors of the document mention Eli in Shiloh as the only priest in possession of the tradition, having received it from the Judges. Samuel was put in a class by himself among the Prophets, as "the Seer."[22] The emphasis on Eli, and therefore on Shiloh as opposed to Jerusalem, suggests hostility to the Jerusalem priesthood. Also noteworthy is the emphasis on Samuel as being the channel through which Eli's tradition came to the Prophets. According to I Chronicles 6.12-13, Elkanah, the father of Samuel, and hence Samuel himself, were Levites. But I Samuel 1.1 describes Elkanah as a native of Mount Ephraim. Eli, in Shiloh, was surely a priest ministering at a sanctuary in the territory of Ephraim. We may thus conjecture that the original document was addressed to the people of the Northern Kingdom and was an effort to win them over to the Prophetic doctrine. It may have been formulated after the fall of that kingdom, or it may date from an earlier time. In either event, it avoided identification of the Prophetic doctrine with loyalty to the Temple in Jerusalem. Any effort to win the northerners to recognition of the Temple in Jerusalem would have met formidable obstacles. Moreover, the Prophets themselves apparently did not recognize the juridical and exegetical authority of the priests in Jerusalem.

In the effort to win the provincials and even the townsmen of the Northern Kingdom to the Prophetic doctrine, it was important to stress that the chain of tradition consisted largely of members of the northern tribes. Thus the fact that Joshua and Samuel both came from Ephraim, and that Shiloh was in that territory, certainly made the proclamation far more attractive to the northerners than it could otherwise have been. From the quotation of Amos in support of the Prophetic authority, it is clear that the authors flourished some generations after him. He had come from the Wilderness of Tekoa, yet apparently he had a following also in northern Israel (Amos 7.1 ff.). Indeed, many of his prophecies concern the Northern Kingdom. It is by no means far fetched to suppose that he founded a school or academy in Israel, and that his disciples, perhaps associated with those of Hosea and other Prophets of northern Israel, claimed authority as spokesmen and interpreters of Torah. The authors of the document, in dissociating themselves completely from the priests in Jerusalem, laid the foundations for the claim later made by the Proto-Pharisees and Pharisees that they were the legitimate successors of Moses.

Apparently, the Prophets claimed that just as Moses, Joshua, and presumably the Elders, the Judges, Eli (I Sam. 4.18), and Samuel (I Sam. 7.15) exercised judicial authority, they, too, as heirs of these teachers, were entitled to do so. A similar claim, of course, was made by the Men of the Great Synagogue (Mishna *Abot* 1.2), and after them by the Pharisaic scholars. The claim of the Proto-Pharisees was made in an addendum to the original document. Seizing on the old tradition, both because of its antiquity and because it paid special respect to Eli of Shiloh and to Samuel, the scholars who flourished after the time of Ezra proclaimed themselves heirs to the Men of the Great Synagogue, to Haggai, Zechariah, and Malachi, and through them to the pre-Exilic Prophets. The claim of the Prophets and the Pharisaic scholars to final judicial authority could be based on the statement in Deuteronomy 17.9 authorizing anyone in doubt as to the law to turn to "the priests, the Levites, *and unto the judge* that shall be in those days." The letter *vav* rendered "and" may also mean "or." Thus the questioner might be considered authorized to turn to the Prophet, or, in later times, to a Pharisaic teacher for instruction.

The Shammaitic editors of ARN I, while still proclaiming the authority of the Men of the Great Synagogue as the heirs of Moses, expunged the name of Eli, the priest of Shiloh, from the chain of tradition leading from the Father of Prophecy to their own generation. They likewise objected to the special place given Samuel the Levite among the Prophets.

As reconstructed on the basis of the comparison of the various versions now extant, the opening section of Mishna *Abot* turns out to be a document originating before the Exile, and establishing the claim of the Prophets as exegetes, scholars, and expounders of the Law.

APPENDIX A TO CHAPTER II

The passage in *Tosefta Berakot* while, as indicated, based on that of *Sifre*, remains challenging. What precisely were "words of wisdom"? The problem is complicated rather than illuminated by the parallel versions of this *baraita* found in *Yer. Berakot* 5.1, 8d; and in *B. ibid.* 31a. *Yerushalmi* substitutes for "wisdom" the word "Torah." *Babli* reads "out of *the joy of Torah.*" (See the discussion of the variant readings and of the text of *Tosefta* in Professor Saul Lieberman's *Tosefta Kifeshutah, ad loc.,* p. 47, and by the late Professor Louis Ginzberg in his *Commentary on the Yerushalmi,* IV, pp. 14 ff.).

The rule was enunciated in a still different form in a *baraita* in *B. Berakot* 31a. This *baraita* holds that "one may not begin to pray in the midst of a legal argument or in the midst of an halakic discussion; but only immediately after [the repetition of] a generally accepted rule."

There is abundant evidence that the norm originally read "words of wisdom" as *Tosefta* has it. This seems likely *a priori,* for while one can well understand how a transmitter, desiring to be precise, might replace "words of wisdom" with "words of Torah," it is unlikely that anyone having learned a rule requiring the recital of "words of Torah" would substitute for that expression "words of wisdom."

This assumption is confirmed by a statement ascribed in *Yerushalmi* (*loc. cit.*) to R. Hoshaya, a teacher of the third century C.E., and in *Babli* (*loc. cit.*) to his disciple, R. Johanan. These teachers recommended the recital before prayer of a *verse from the Psalter* expressing faith in God's protection. Their instruction was adopted by all rituals of later times, so that according to every known ritual, morning, afternoon, and evening prayers are still preceded by verses from the Psalms.

Presumably R. Hoshaya (who is known to have been associated with the compilation of *Tosefta*) interpreted the word *hokmah* ("wisdom") to mean the Book of Psalms.

Moreover, both he and his disciple, R. Johanan, apparently knew of the relation of the norm in *Tosefta* to the passage of *Sifre* Deuteronomy on which it is based. They therefore held that the verse from the Psalter employed as preparation for prayer should be one of faith and comfort. We shall hereafter discover other evidence (p. 94) that R. Johanan, unlike other scholars of his day, was acquainted with *Sifre* on Deuteronomy, Chapter 33, and particularly with the passage under discussion.

However, as will be shown below (p. 93), the norm of *Tosefta* was by no means unanimously accepted. According to some authorities, prayer should be said not in a mood of hope and faith, but in one of solemnity and even fear of punishment. Public prayer should therefore be preceded by admonition (cf. Mishna *Berakot* 5.1).

The version of the norm under discussion as cited in *Yerushalmi* was deliberately ambiguous. Its editors replaced the word "wisdom" with "Torah" which might mean admonition or encouragement and consolation. The Babylonian authorities, seeking to reconcile current practice with the altered form of the norm, changed it still further to "the joy of Torah."

Earlier authorities, endeavoring to reconcile the version of the norm as cited in *Yerushalmi* (but doubtless deriving from Tannaitic times) with that found in *Tosefta,* concluded that *Tosefta* employed the word *hokmah* to indicate that the preliminaries for prayer may not consist of arguments about the Law. Such arguments might well interfere with concentration on prayer. Torah and Wisdom meant, they held, a rule of the Law, contemplation of which would put one in the frame of mind needed for prayer. This view is reflected in the *baraita* cited in *B. Berakot* 31a.

As the halakist understood the passage in *Sifre,* it recommended that prayer should follow the recitation of some verses or some discussion which helped men to have faith in Divine assistance. That is why the Prophets did not resort to admonition before prayer, but rather to words of "praise," *i.e.,* praise of God as Deliverer of Israel, and "consolation," *viz.* comfort, showing that one could rely on His help. The Book of Psalms was an eminent example of such words of praise and comfort. Therefore, to this day all synagogue services begin with a recital of passages from the Psalms. This is true even of the penitential prayers recited early in the morning each weekday between Rosh ha-Shanah and Yom Kippur, and for some days before Rosh ha-Shanah. It seems obvious that the halakist thought of the Psalter as "words of wisdom," rather than as Prophecy. Other teachers in *B.* and *Yer. Berakot, loc. cit.*, identified words of wisdom with the Pharisaic tradition, a meaning which the term *hokmah* often has (*cf.* the discussions of Professors Ginzberg and Lieberman, *loc. cit.*).

The opposing view, namely, that one prays more fervently after rebuke and exhortation, is reflected in Mishna *Berakot* 5.1, which, like the passage cited from *B. Berakot* 31a, was opposed to the norm cited regarding words of wisdom (*cf.*, however, *Tosafot, ad loc.*, catchword, *Rab Ashi.*) The view of Mishna *Berakot* 5.1 was also shared by the authors of Mishna *Ta'anit* 2.1, which required an Elder to say words of exhortation before the special prayers of the day. It is reported that Hillel, on one occasion, when he was present at the ceremony of the water-libations on Sukkot, saw the people turning to pray in the midst of frivolity. He rebuked them, reminding them that God had no need for their praise. When he saw that "their hearts were broken" through his words, he added, "Although He has thousands and myriads of myriads of Angels of the Service, He desires only the praise of Israel." Thus he prepared them for prayer through words of consolation, in accordance with the norm cited above, and following the implications it drew from *Sifre.* (ARN II Chap. 27, 28a; another version, in which the point is obscured, is found in *Yer. Sukkah* 5.4, 55b.)

APPENDIX B TO CHAPTER II

In the discussion in *Yerushalmi* (*Berakot* 5. 1, 8d) of the norm requiring one to rise to pray only after hearing words of Torah, "just as the early Prophets ended their remarks with words of praise and consolation," R. Eleazar remarked, "except for Jeremiah, who ended with words of reproof," predicting the fall of Babylonia. To this, R. Johanan replied that Jeremiah was not an exception to the rule; he ended his Book with the prediction of the fall of Babylonia, "because he had prophesied the destruction of those who had destroyed the Temple.[1] Lest therefore you suppose that he concluded with a prophecy concerning the destruction of the Temple, Scripture says, 'Thus far are the words of Jeremiah' " (Jer. 51.64). (This verse follows the statement "And thou shalt say, 'Thus shall Babylon sink, and shall not rise again, because of the evil I will bring upon her; and they shall be weary.' ") "He spoke of the fall of the destroyers of the Temple. He did not end with words of reproof."

It is clear that R. Eleazer did not know the passage in *Sifre* Deuteronomy on which the norm is based. Otherwise he could not have asked the question for *Sifre* Deuteronomy specifically includes Jeremiah among the Prophets whose words ended with words of comfort. R. Johanan did know the passage in *Sifre* (see above, p. 92). However, he felt compelled to emend it, because *Sifre* Deuteronomy (as we have seen above, p. 13) cites Jeremiah, Chapter 31, as proof for its thesis, whereas R. Johanan knew the Book of Jeremiah as we now have it. Therefore, he changed the traditional text through the addition of the statement given above, and which in altered form has been incorporated into the *Sifre* as now extant.

Significantly, R. Eleazer, born in Babylonia, included among "words of rebuke" a threat against a Gentile nation; whereas R. Johanan, a native of the land of Israel, realized that the author of the homily of *Sifre* had in mind only Prophetic reproof and admonition to Israel, as well as consolation and comfort to Israel.

APPENDIX A TO CHAPTER IX
The Presence of the Donor at a Sacrifice

The issue whether a donor was required to be present at the offering of his sacrifice deserves more extensive discussion than was possible in the text. According to *B. Sotah* 8a, the same principle underlay the rule requiring a suspected wife to be present at the Temple for the prescribed ordeal.

Rashi, apparently recognizing the rejection of the implied postulate of Mishna *Ta'anit* 4.2 by later authorities, sought support for the Talmudic comment of *B. Sotah* 8a in *Sifre* Numbers 142. *Sifre,* he believed, reflected the consensus of the rabbis; and apparently *B. Sotah* 8a was extending to private offerings the principle suggested in *Sifre* for public sacrifices.

While Maimonides in his Code (*Hilkot Kle ha-Miqdash* 6.1) quotes the passage of Mishna *Ta'anit* 4.2, he nowhere requires an individual to be present at the offering of his sacrifices. And indeed no such rule was mentioned in the Pentateuch. Rabbi Meir Simhah of Dvinsk (*Or Sameah* on Maim. Code, *loc. cit.*), seeking a source for the norm of Mishna *Ta'anit* 4.2, found it in the rule which imposed on the prince about to offer a sacrifice the duty of standing at the gate of the Temple during the ceremony (Ezek. 46.2).

Various passages do, indeed, seem to require that one offering a sacrifice bring it personally to the Temple (Mishna *Bikkurim* 1.9; *Tosefta Peah* 4.7, ed. Lieberman p. 57; *Sifre* Deut. 77, p. 142; *cf. Sifre* Num. 29, p. 36; *Sifra Nedabah, par.* 3.13, 5c; *ibid. Hobah, perek* 18.4, 24c; *ibid. Tazria, perek* 3.4, 59b; *Mekilta of R. Simeon* 23.19, p. 219; *ibid.* 34.26, p. 224). But traditionally these were interpreted to mean only that the owner of the sacrifice had to r*eplace* the animal with another if lost. At least, this was the interpretation which R. Judah appears to have put on the norm; for he added (*Sifre* Deuteronomy, *loc. cit.*): "He is only responsible for the animal until he brings it to the Well of the Golah" (*i.e.,* to the borders of the Court of the Temple).

Only in regard to sacrificial animals set aside outside the land of Israel (see *Sifre* Deuteronomy, *loc. cit.*), did Maimonides hold that the owner himself was bound, by a positive commandment, to bring the animal to the Temple (see Maim., *Ma'aseh ha-Qorbanot,* Chap. 18, beg.). He held this view despite the fact that the language used in *Sifra Nedabah* (*loc. cit.*) suggested that the rule applied to all sacrificial animals.

But none of these norms obliged the owner to be present when the ritual of the sacrifices was performed, and it seems improbable that they were understood in that sense. (See the authorities and references cited by Professor Saul Lieberman in *Tosefta Kifeshutah, Bikkurim,* pp. 829 ff. It seems probable that *Tosefta Peah* 4.7 originally read, "He is under obligation to take the trouble to bring them to the Temple." But transmitters, who held that he had only an obligation to see to it that they were brought to the Temple, whether he brought them himself or sent them through an agent, emended the text. They added the word "responsibility," and it now reads: "He is responsible for the trouble of bringing them to the Temple.")

The assumption of Mishna *Ta'anit* 4.2, that a donor must be present at the time of sacrifice, is not only generally ignored in the Talmud, but some passages actually contradict it. Thus Mishna *Gittin* 3.3 provides that a sin-offering, sent to the Temple from a distant country (*medinat ha-yam,* "a country of the sea"), may be sacrificed on the altar on the assumption that the donor was still living. This assumption was necessary because, according to prevailing Mishnaic law, a sin-offering could not be sacrificed posthumously (Mishna *Temurah* 2.2). Therefore, one might well apprehend that a sin-offering sent from a distant country was being sacrificed after the unreported death of the donor. The norm implies that other sacrifices, not subject to this restriction, may, *a fortiori,* be offered in the absence of the donor.

The Babylonian Talmud (*ad loc.*) simply asks how the norm of the Mishna is to be reconciled with the Pentateuchal commandment that one bringing a sacrifice put his hands upon it before it is offered on the altar (Lev. 4.4). The Talmud does not ask how the norm of Mishna *Gittin* 3.3 can be reconciled with Mishna *Ta'anit* 4.2, indicating that Mishna *Ta'anit* was not regarded as setting down a positive rule applying to all sacrifices. The Talmud of Jerusalem does not even raise the question of the inconsistency of Mishna *Gittin* 3.3 with the Pentateuchal requirement of s*emikah* (the ritual of leaning on the animal before it is sacrificed). The reason for this omission is that the Talmud of Jerusalem considers the ceremony of *semikah* commendable, but not indispensable to the validity of the sacrifice (Mishna *Menahot* 9.8; *Sifra Nedabah, perek* 4, end, 6a).

Indeed, in his revised commentary on Mishna *Ta'anit.*

4.2, Rashi explained that the presence of a donor at the offering of his sacrifice was needed to comply with the rule stated in Leviticus 1.4; 3.3; 4.4, 15, 24, 29, 33. These verses command a donor of a sacrifice to lay his hands on it. (This passage of Rashi's revised commentary is not found in the current text, but is quoted by Rabbi Solomon Adeni in his Commentary on the Mishna, called *Meleket Shelomoh, loc. cit.*). Thus Rashi knew of no rule taking it for granted that a donor had to be present near his sacrifice, other than for the ritual of leaning on the animal. In fact, it can be shown that the assumption of Mishna *Ta'anit* 4.2 that a donor must be present at the offering of his sacrifice, was rejected by virtually the whole Talmudic tradition.

Something must have occurred between the time of the composition of Mishna *Ta'anit* 4.2, where the presence of a donor is taken as a matter of course, and of *Tosefta* on this very passage which, like the rest of the Talmud, lacks any reference to this rule.

B. Menahot 62b quotes a Tannaitic source stating that the ritual of waving the prescribed portions of a sacrifice sent by a donor in a distant land may be performed on his behalf by the ministering priest. Nothing is said in that context about the impropriety of offering the sacrifice in the donor's absence. Again the Talmud fails to note the incompatibility of the norm with Mishna *Ta'anit* 4.2.

Tosefta Hagigah 1.1 derives the rule freeing a defiled person from the duty of sending an offering to the Temple at the time of the festival, from the verse, "But into the place which the Lord, your God, shall choose out of all your tribes to put His name there, even unto His habitation shall ye seek *and thither thou shalt come; and thither* ye shall bring your burnt offerings. . . ." (Deut. 12.5, 6). *Tosefta* infers from this verse that only those permitted to enter the Temple precincts were required to bring sacrifices to it. Being barred from the Temple, a defiled person was under no obligation *to send* a sacrifice at festival time. *Tosefta* in this passage (cited also in *B. Hagigah* 4b. and *Yer. Hagigah* 1.4, 76a) seems to imply that a donor who is not defiled *may send* his sacrifice to the Temple to be offered in his absence.

Several passages dealing with the absent donor indicate that the change in Jewish life affecting the ancient rule was the emergence of the Diaspora. The rise of the Diaspora inevitably necessitated revision of the principle of Mishna *Ta'anit* 4.2. That Mishna was formulated when almost all Israelites dwelt in the Holy Land or in neighbouring countries such as Moab, Edom, Ammon, and Zidon. With the development of Diasporas in more distant countries, the rule had to be relaxed. A Jew living in a distant country might conceivably go to Jerusalem, purchase his sacrificial animal there, and take it to the Temple. But circumstances might prevent him from making the journey and, in that event, he might prefer to choose the beast in his home town, and send it with someone else, or he might authorize an agent to purchase a sacrificial animal on his behalf in Jerusalem.

In the light of the new custom, the question also arose whether one defiled, although his impurity would bar him from attendance at the Temple could send a sacrifice.

Thus, a person, falling ill in a country far from Jerusalem, unable to travel there and fearing that his illness had come upon him in punishment for a specific transgression, might wish to choose a favourite animal for sacrifice as a sin-offering and send it to the Temple through an agent. As I have shown elsewhere (*Albeck Jubilee Vol.* pp. 357 ff.), the Shammaites held that the donor of a sacrifice, especially of a sin-offering, was obliged to set it aside, to "sanctify" it. Therefore the transgressor, concerned for his atonement, would choose the sacrificial beast in his home city and send it to Jerusalem through his son, or a slave, or an agent.

That was, in fact, why *Sifra* on Leviticus 1.4 remarked that the ceremony of putting one's hands on the head of the sacrificial beast might not be performed on one's behalf by one's son, one's slave, or one's agent. No such rule would be necessary if all sacrifices had to be offered in the presence of the donor; the donor would perform the ceremony himself. But the question arose: If he were away, and had sent the sacrifice through his son, a slave or an agent, could anyone lay hands on the animal in his behalf? *Sifra,* and following it Mishna *Menahot* 9.8, (which omits the word for "one's son" and replaces it with "one's wife") declares that the ritual of laying hands on the head of the sacrifice is a commandment which may be performed only by the donor himself.

Another historical development which may have affected the attitude of the ancient scholars to the requirement of the donor's presence during a sacrifice was the problem of offerings made by pagans. Whatever may have been the rule in pre-Exilic times, in Rabbinic law pagans were forbidden to enter the Temple precincts (Mishna *Kelim* 1.8), but they could donate sacrificial offerings (*B. Hullin* 5a; Mishna *Sheqalim* 1.8, according to the usual texts; the passage is missing in ed. Lowe and several authoritative mss.).

The question of the acceptance of sacrifices by Gentiles would hardly have arisen before the centralization of worship in Jerusalem; probably not before the Restoration. The Persian government itself contributed sacrifices to the re-established Temple (*cf.*, Ezra 6.9, mentioning sacrifices to be contributed by the government on behalf of the Great King). Significantly, King Solomon, in his prayer at the dedication of the Temple (I Kgs. 8.41, 42), spoke of Gentiles offering prayers in the Temple, but not of any sacrifices offered by them. The author of the prayer evidently held that pagans could enter the Temple precincts.

The acceptance of sacrifices from pagans, forbidden to enter the Temple, and the problem arising out of the Diaspora, combined to introduce a new concept in sacrifice; namely, that it could be offered in the absence of the donor.

The change of attitude toward the rule requiring the actual presence of a donor at the offering of his sacrifice can be traced also through the different interpretations put on Deuteronomy 12.26, "Only thy holy things which thou hast, and thy vows thou shalt take, and go unto the place which the Lord shall choose." *Sifre* Deuteronomy 77 (p. 142) on this passage, states: "What is the verse discussing? The sacrifices coming from the Holy Land, have already been mentioned (Deut. 12.11). Therefore the verse deals only with sacrifices from other lands. '*Thou shall take and go.*' [This passage teaches] that he [the donor] is obliged to take charge of them (*i.e.*, the sacrificial animals) until he brings them to the Temple." After discussion of the various types of sacrifices to which the rule applied, *Sifre* continues: "R. Akiba said: 'The verse deals with animals given in exchange [contrary to the law of Leviticus 20.10] for others originally designated for the sacrifice.'" The same interpretation was put on the verse by R. Akiba's colleague, R. Ishmael (*ibid.* 78, p. 144). It seems clear that both R. Ishmael and R. Akiba based their views on those of their teachers, who had taken the verse to refer to animals given in exchange for those originally marked for sacrifice.

But why did these later Sages insist that the verse discussed such an unusual circumstance as the forbidden exchange of one beast for another? The answer is that the older interpretation was no longer acceptable. The view that an animal designated for sacrifice outside the Holy Land had to be taken to Jerusalem by the owner himself, could be maintained only when neighbouring countries were involved. The rule could not possibly be maintained when the distant Diasporas developed. Under those circumstances, the donor could not be obligated to take the sacrificial animal to Jerusalem himself. If he designated a beast for sacrifice, he could send it through another man, as Mishna *Gittin* 3.3 and the other passages mentioned above imply. It may be significant that in both passages discussing sacrifices sent through agents, the word for foreign country is not the usual *huzzah la'arez* ("outside the land"); but *medinat ha-yam* ("distant countries approached through the sea"), such as Asia Minor, the Greek Islands, Greece, and even Rome.

At a very early time the original passage in *Sifre* itself came to be interpreted in accord with later views. Thus *Tosefta Peah* 4.7 (ed. Zuckermandel p. 23; ed. Lieberman p. 57) paraphrases the statement of *Sifre* as follows: "For the holy things *of the Sanctuary* [in contrast with the heave-offering which is the holy thing of the provinces] one is responsible and *one must see that they are delivered to the Temple.*" *Tosefta* recognized that the owner need not himself take the sacrificial beast to the Temple. He was responsible only to insure its safe arrival or to its replacement if lost.

In contrast to the sacrificial animals, the heave-offering was not necessarily taken to the Temple or to the priest;

the priest went to the granary to collect it, as Professor Saul Lieberman explains in his comment on *Tosefta Terumot* 10.17 (*see Tosefta Kifeshutah*, p. 478).

The anonymous comment in *Sifre* Deuteronomy 77, commanding the worshipper dwelling outside the Holy Land to take a beast set aside for sacrifice to the Temple himself, probably derives from approximately the same period as Mishna *Ta'anit* 4.2. Its assumption is that the donor should himself be present at the sacrifice. The various parallel passages in *Sifra* and *Sifre* Numbers may be quotations from *Sifre* Deuteronomy 77, rather than independent comments on the verses to which they are attached. If they were meant to be taken literally, there would be no need to insist in various parts of *Sifra* that the owner alone may put his hands on the head of the beast.

Therefore, the anonymous statement of *Sifre* Deuteronomy 77 is probably part of a document which, like Mishna *Ta'anit* 4.2, is of pre-Exilic origin. In the final generation of the First Commonwealth, there was already a considerable Diaspora in existence—not, indeed, in "the lands of the sea," but in the neighbouring countries, particularly Egypt. Donors dwelling in those countries, who had designated animals for sacrificial purposes, were required to take them to the Temple.

APPENDIX B TO CHAPTER IX

In addition to the lists of priestly families mentioned in the text (pp. 60 ff.), we must take into account that found in Nehemiah 12.1 ff., which enumerates the clans that returned with Zerubabel. This record is quite different from that found in *Tosefta*, Ezra 2.36 ff., and Nehemiah 7.39 ff. The list in Nehemiah 12.1 ff., mentions not four, but twenty-two families.

It is repeated in Nehemiah 12.12 ff., giving the names of the heads of each group during the high priesthood of Joiakim, the son of Jeshua, who had been first High Priest of the restored community. The second list contains only twenty-one names. In both lists Jehoiarib is the seventeenth clan, Jedaiah the eighteenth. Immer appears as Amariah in the fourth place. Harim, mentioned in the second list, apparently is identical with the one called Rehum in the first list. Pashhur is omitted in these lists, but perhaps it was replaced with that of Maloki (Neh. 12.14), which may be a variant for the name Malkiah, occurring as one of the priestly subdivisions in I Chronicles 24.9 ff. In Nehemiah 12.2, the name Maluki is written Maluk, which is a separate group according to Nehemiah 10.5. However, the spelling, Maluk, in Nehemiah 12.2 may be erroneous. This family is mentioned immediately after Immer.

It is more probable that the name Maloki replaced that of Pashhur in the lists in Nehemiah, Chapter 12, since in the account in Nehemiah 11.12 and I Chronicles 9.12, Pashhur is called the son of Malkiah. Perhaps this genealogy represents an effort on the part of the clan of Pashhur to obtain identification for itself free from the traditional blame attaching to its eponym, for Pashhur is described in Jeremiah 20.1 as an opponent of the Prophet, and was the object of a Prophetic condemnation (*ibid*. v. 6).

Moreover, the name Seraiah, which is the first of the families listed in Nehemiah 12.1 ff., and 12.12 ff., probably stands for the leading family of the clan of Jedaiah. The name Seraiah was given this family because Seraiah was the last priest of the Solomonic Temple, and probably belonged to the clan of Jedaiah (*cf.*, Neh. 11.11; II Kgs. 25.18). The name Jedaiah, which occurs later in the list, therefore signifies another branch of the same clan, not directly descended from the former High Priest Seraiah.

If in Nehemiah, Chapter 12, Seraiah represents the leading family of the clan of Jedaiah, the order of the four clans in Nehemiah 12.1 ff., and 12.12 ff., while interspersed with other names, is identical with that of Ezra 2.36 ff. and Nehemiah 7.39 ff., *viz.* Seraiah (which according to this explanation is the *real* Jedaiah); Amariah, to be identified with Immer, fourth; Maloki (called Maluk in Nehemiah 12.2), to be identified with Pashhur, fifth; Harim (written Rehum in Nehemiah 12.3), seventh (in the second list, which does not mention the clan of Hattush, and eighth in the first, which does).

The order of priority of the main families in relation to one another would therefore be in this list as in the others mentioned: Jedaiah, Immer, Pashhur, Harim.

Among the signers of the Great Document in Nehemiah, Chapters 9 and 10, again twenty-two priestly clans are mentioned. Not all are identical with those of Nehemiah, Chapter 12, but they do include Seraiah, Pashhur, Amariah, Malkiah, and Harim, in that order, although interspersed with others. If we take it that Malkiah in this list represents the original Pashhur (which had changed its name) the order becomes identical with that of the other lists in Ezra and Nehemiah, so far discussed, *viz.*, Jedaiah, Immer, Pashhur, and Harim.

APPENDIX C TO CHAPTER IX
The Meaning of the Term 'Ma'amad' in Various Contexts

In the final generations of the Second Commonwealth, the term *ma'amad* was employed in the sense given it in *Tosefta*, *i.e.*, meaning only Israelites representing specific areas, but not priests and Levites. Thus, each day an announcer at the Temple would summon "the priests to their ministry, the Levites to their platform [where they performed the ministry of song], and the Israelites to their *ma'amad*," (*Yer. Sheqalim* 5.2, 48d. ed. A. Sofer p. 58; *B. Yoma* 20b). The officials of the Temple enumerated in Mishna *Sheqalim* 5.2, and discussed in *Yer. loc. cit.*, were those of the last generation of the Second Temple, contemporaries of King Agrippa II. (See *Yer. Sheqalim* and *B. Yoma, loc. cit.;* as well as J. N. Epstein, *Mebuot le-Sifrut ha-Tannaim,* ed. E. Z. Melammed, p. 25). The phrase "the priests in their ministry, the Levites on their platform, and the Israelites in their *ma'amad*" is also quoted several times in the Babylonian Talmud. Thus in *B. Zebahim* 19a, a Tannaitic source is cited as holding that "the priests engaged in their ministry, the Levites standing on their platform [and engaged in the ministry of song], and the Israelites at their *ma'amad* are free from the duty of praying or donning the phylacteries." On the other hand, according to *B. Megillah* 3a all three groups were obliged to hear the reading of the Scroll of Esther on Purim. *B. Yoma* 53a records that all three groups, having completed their duty, left the Temple area walking sideways, neither turning their backs on the Temple nor walking backwards.

According to *Sifre* Numbers 142 (p. 188), the *ma'amadot* consisted of priests, Levites, and Israelites. The passage offers an interpretation of the command in Numbers 28.2, "My food which is presented unto Me, for offerings made by fire, of a sweet savour unto Me, *shall ye observe* [or rather, 'shall ye heed'] to offer unto Me in its due season." The word *tishmeru,* rendered "shall heed," is taken by *Sifre* (as it is by *Tosefta, loc. cit.*) to require representatives of the people to be present at the public sacrifices enumerated in that chapter of Numbers.

Thus, whereas according to *Tosefta* these representatives consisted of Israelites only, *Sifre* states that the verse implies that "priests, Levites, and Israelites should stand over it [the sacrifice]."

Tosefta Ta'anit 3(4)3 (p. 337) ends with the citation of the remark of R. Simeon ben Eleazar that "the priests, the Levites, the musical instruments, *and the people (ve-ha'am)* are indispensable to the sacrifice." (For the word *ve-ha'am,* the parallel passages in *B. Ta'anit* 27a, ed. Malter p. 126, *Yer. ibid.* 4.2, 67d, read "Israelites," see Professor Saul Lieberman in *Tosefta Kifeshutah, ad loc. Ta'anit,* p. 1104). It is clear from this passage that the priests and Levites were considered indispensable, but this was not because of their respective ministries. That would not have required any remark by R. Simeon ben Eleazar. He was rather insisting that all three groups had *to be present* in the *ma'amadot.* (For a further discussion of this divergence of opinion see Professor Saul Lieberman in *Tosefta Kifeshutah, loc. cit.,* and H. Malter, *Ta'anit,* p. 120.).

It may be that the tradition preserved in *Sifre* Numbers followed the views of the non-priests who adhered to the ancient practice, commanded in the Mishna, requiring the *ma'amadot* at the Temple to include priests and Levites as well as Israelites. On the other hand, *Tosefta,* rejecting that teaching, may record the tradition of the Temple priests themselves.

That there was such a difference of view between priests and lay scholars seems implied in the fact that the Temple officials, who were priests, used the word *ma'amad*, as we have seen, for Israelites only. Moreover, there appears to have existed a controversy with regard to the propriety of priests, Levites, and Israelites engaged in their respective duties at the Temple (the priests and Levites in their ministries and the Israelites at the *ma'amad*) donning phylacteries. As above noted, *B. Zebahim* 19a preserves a record according to which all three groups are free from the duty of wearing phylacteries or reciting the prayers.

On the other hand, the Talmud transmits another tradition, according to which at least some priests wore *tephillin* while engaged in the Temple service. Those who accepted this tradition must have required the Levites and the Israelites present at the Temple to don *tephillin*.

In its effort to reconcile the two traditions, the Talmud draws a distinction between the *tephillin* worn on the arm and those worn on the head. The former apparently could not be donned by the priests while they wore their holy garments, for the *tephillin* on the arm would separate the tunic from the priest's body, which was contrary to the rule that the tunic must be placed immediately on the body of the priest.

Presumably, however, the two traditions were originally independent. Hence, the discussion in *B. Arakin* 3b ignores completely the view that the priests, Levites, and Israelites worshipping in the Temple were free from the obligation to don the *tephillin*. Maimonides in his Code (*Hilkot Kle ha-Miqdash* 10.6) simply states that a priest may not wear *tephillin* on his *arm* while he is engaged in his ministry; but "if he wishes to wear the *tephillin* on his head during his ministry, he may do so." The formulation of this statement suggests that Maimonides perceived that two opposing customs regarding phylacteries prevailed in the Temple. In this closing remark, without mentioning the principle applying to the Levites and Israelites, he hints at the tradition according to which none of the priests, Levites, and Israelites engaged in the Temple service during their special term of ministry were required to don the *tephillin* or to recite the prayers.

We would be justified in the assumption that the priestly tradition freed the priests from the obligation of wearing *tephillin* or engaging in prayer during the term of their ministry at the Temple. The opposing tradition apparently required them, as well as the Levites and the Israelites of the *ma'amad,* to don the *tephillin* and to recite the prayers. While some priests followed the tradition deriving from non-priestly authorities, most of them probably did not.

Thus neither Mishna *Tamid* 5.1 (ed. A. Brody, p. 76), describing the daily liturgy of the priests, nor Mishna *Yoma,* recording in detail the ceremonies of the Day of Atonement in the Temple, mention the recital of the prayers. They clearly imply that the usual prayers of the synagogue were not recited by the priests in the Temple.

While *Sifre* and *Tosefta* disagree regarding the constituency of the *ma'amadot,* in neither is the word *ma'amadot* employed in the sense of local, regional gatherings. Both assumed that the priests and Levites worshipped according to their organization as clans, following the order fixed in earlier times.

APPENDIX D TO CHAPTER IX
The Order of the Priestly Clans in the Final Years of the Second Temple

Almost all records regarding the order of service by the priestly clans indicate that Jehoiarib ministered during the week beginning with the first Sabbath in the first month, *i.e.,* Nisan, (see above, p. 63). However, one passage in *Tosefta Ta'anit* 3(4).9 (ed. Zuckermandel p. 220; ed. Lieberman p. 340) states: "The Temple was destroyed for the first time [i.e. in the year 586 B.C.E.] on the evening following the Sabbath, in the year following the Sabbatical year, *during the ministry of Jehoiarib,* on the ninth of Ab.[1] And *this happened likewise* in the destruction of the Second Temple." (See ed. Lieberman and his *Tosefta Kifeshutah, ibid.* p. 1077, for references to parallel passages.)

The Talmud (*B. Arakin* 12b) is at great pains to reconcile this statement with those cited above (p. 58), which it interprets as meaning that Jehoiarib did not return from the Exile at all. Professor Saul Lieberman has pointed out that *Yerushalmi*, quoting this passage, does not raise the question. On the contrary, *Yerushalmi* assumes in various passages that Jehoiarib was the first of the ministering families each year (see *Tosefta Kifeshutah, loc. cit.*).

Similarly, a passage in *Vayyikra R.* 28.2 (ed. Margoliot, p. 653) specifically asserts that the clans of Jeshua and Shekaniah always ministered about the time of Shabuot. This could only be if Jehoiarib always ministered during the first week in Nisan (see the note of Professor Saul Lieberman, *ad loc.*, p. 879). As already noted above (p. 63), the calendar of the Qumran community likewise takes it for granted that Jehoiarib ministered during the first full week of Nisan and Tishri.

Yet it seems clear that at some time Jehoiarib's term of ministry occurred early in the month of Ab. The change may conceivably have been made in order to confer a special advantage on Jehoiarib. The ninth of Ab was a great festival for many families, who brought wood for the altar at this time. (Mishna *Ta'anit* 4.5; ed. Malter, p. 121; *cf.*, notes of Ch. Albeck, in his ed., p. 597; J. N. Epstein, *Mabo le-Nusah ha-Mishnah*, p. 1211; *Tosefta Bikkurim* 2.9, ed. Lieberman p. 292, and his *Tosefta Kifeshutah, ad loc.*, and references there given.)

More probably the change was made in the final days of the Temple, when the High Priest was chosen by lot (Josephus, *War*, IV 3.8; *cf. Sifra Emor, par.* 2.1, 94c; *Tosefta Yoma* 1.6, ed. Lieberman p. 222); and when perhaps other revolutionary measures were adopted. We may speculate that the change in the time of the ministry of Jehoiarib was part of a new system of rotation among the priestly clans. We have seen (p. 62) what advantages accrued to the clans which had the right to minister during the Passover week or near it; and, presumably, also during the Sukkot week or near it. The urge to democratic rule among the priests, which led to the selection of a High Priest through a lottery might very well have induced the priests to institute a new order of ministry among themselves. In this new order, the twenty-four clans served in rotation. When they had all served, a new cycle began, precisely as Maimonides states in his Code (*Hilkot Kle ha-Miqdash* 4.3). But this meant that Jehoiarib, which ministered during the first week of Nisan in the first year, necessarily served earlier the next year, and still earlier the next. If an intercalary month was added, Jehoiarib found its term of ministry set back by four weeks more.

Thus if Jehoiarib, before the change was made, had ministered in the first month of Nisan and the first month of Tishri, it served its second term about the middle of Elul in the second year; in the second half of Ab in the third year; and probably during the first week of Ab in the fourth year.

A simple calculation will show why, in the fourth year after the introduction of this new system of rotation of clans, the term of Jehoiarib began on Saturday, the first of Ab.

As already observed, according to *Tosefta Ta'anit, loc. cit.*, in the year of the destruction of the Temple the ninth of Ab occurred on a Sunday. Therefore the first of Ab in that year occurred on a Saturday. Usually 118 days separate the first of Ab from the first of Nisan (two months of thirty days and two of twenty-nine days[2]). If the new system of rotation of priestly clans had been inaugurated three years before Nisan of the year 70 C.E. (when the Temple was destroyed), the time which had elapsed between Nisan I of the year I[3] (when the new system was inaugurated) and Nisan I of the year IV (three years later) might have been 1062, 1063, 1064 or 1065 days. The number would depend upon the number of days in those years. If the three years each had 355 days, the total would be 1065; if one had 354, the total would be 1064; if two had 354 the total would be 1063; or if all three had 354 days, the total would be 1062. Thus, the time between Nisan I of Year I and Ab I of Year IV would be either 1183, 1182, 1181, or 1180 days.

If the total was 1183 days, the time would add up to exactly 169 weeks; if 1182, to 168 weeks plus six days; if 1181, to 168 weeks plus five days; if 1180, to 168 weeks plus four days.[4] As the first of Ab in Year IV occurred on Saturday, if the total was 1183 days, the first of Nisan in Year I also occurred on Saturday.[5] If the total was 1182, the first of Nisan in Year I occurred on a Sunday; if 1181, on Monday; if 1180, on Tuesday.

108

In any event, the ministry of Jehoiarib would begin either on the Sabbath which was the first of Nisan of Year I or on the Sabbath following the first of Nisan. If the ministry of Jehoiarib began on the Sabbath following the New Moon of Nisan of Year I, the 168 weeks elapsing between that Sabbath and the first of Ab of Year IV would account for seven rotations of the priestly cycle.[6] Its new term would begin on the first of Ab in Year IV, and it would serve until the eighth of Ab of that year. Apparently, that is precisely what happened. As the term of the ministry of Jehoiarib drew to its end on the eighth of Ab, the Romans broke into the Temple, robbing it of its utensils and preparing to set it afire.[7] Thus, the Temple was burnt on the following evening, the ninth of Ab, which was still called the time of Jehoiarib; for that group could not be replaced by Jedaiah with the Roman soldiers occupying the Sanctuary.

We may speculate even further with some confidence on the reason leading to this change in the order of service of the priestly clans toward the end of the Second Temple. The change may have been caused by the reintroduction of the Law of the Jubilee (Lev. 25.8 ff.) for farm lands. There is clear indication in *Yer. Sukkah*, end, associating the order of the priests, as it seems to have prevailed in the final years of the Second Temple, with the Law of the Jubilee.

The problem posed there is that according to Leviticus 27.22 ff., ancestral land given to the Temple reverts to the priests in the Jubilee year, unless it is redeemed before that. According to the Mishnaic norm, the group of priests to whom such land reverted was that ministering when the Jubilee year began (*B. Arakin* 28b). According to Rashi (*ad loc.*), this meant the clan ministering on the Day of Atonement of the Jubilee year; for the year of the Jubilee was proclaimed on the tenth of Tishri (Lev. 25.9). As observed above (p. 64), the clan ministering each year on the Day of Atonement was originally, in all probability, Jehoiarib.

According to the rule in the Babylonian Talmud, the right to minister during the week when the Day of Atonement occurred had great property value, perhaps far in excess of the advantages, already mentioned, attaching to the ministry immediately before Passover. The reason is as follows: It was by no means uncommon for a landowner to donate land to the Temple. Had the law of the Jubilee year been followed, all agricultural land would have been subject to the norms of Leviticus 27.22 ff. That is, land given to the Temple and not redeemed by the original owner before the Jubilee would become the property of the priests ministering in the Temple on the Day of Atonement in the Jubilee year. Originally, in all probability, this would be the clan of Jehoiarib.

However, *Yer. Sukkah,* end, takes for granted a system by which the clan ministering on the Day of Atonement was not the same year after year, and the privilege rotated among the various clans; the reason for this rotation being the right of the clan ministering at that season to obtain the land given the Temple during the Jubilee year.

As we have observed, at one time the clan of Jehoiarib always ministered during the first week of Nisan. Therefore, the clans ministering during the other weeks would also be the same each year. Thus it is clear that *Yer. Sukkah,* end, refers to an innovation, possibly introduced during the final years of the Temple.

APPENDIX E TO CHAPTER IX

Another norm dealing with the *ma'amadot* is apparently likewise of very early origin, although later than the passage in Mishna *Ta'anit,* just discussed. But like the Mishna, this norm appears to demonstrate the very early origin of the system of *ma'amadot.* The norm reads: "One who recites the *Shema'* with the men of the *mishmar* [the priests serving in the Temple during their assigned week] does not fulfill his obligation, for they recite the *Shema'* too early. One who recites the *Shema'* with the men of the *ma'amad* does not fulfill his duty, for they recite it after the assigned time."

The authors of this norm agreed with the scholars who maintained that the *Shema'* ought to be recited precisely at sunrise. The priests of the *mishmar,* as Mishna *Tamid* (5.1) records, recited the *Shema'* long before sunrise because their

110

time afterward was fully occupied with the ritual of the daily sacrifices.

But why did not the men of the *ma'amad* read the *Shema'* on time? The commentators have, in general, taken it for granted that the *ma'amad* under discussion was the representation of the Israelites in Jerusalem, because the term is used in that sense in most passages of the Mishna, and in other Rabbinic works stemming from the last generations of the Second Commonwealth. However, these Israelites in Jerusalem surely could have found time to recite the *Shema'* at its proper hour, or at the same time as the ministering priests, before the Temple service. Professor Louis Ginzberg, in his *Commentary on the Yerushalmi* I (p. 78 ff.), assumes that the men of the *ma'amad* at the Temple were busy preparing wood for the altar and in similar occupations relating to the service. But this seems far fetched. More probably, the word *ma'amad* is used in this norm in the sense it has in the oldest sources discussing the system of *mishmarot*, such as Mishna *Ta'anit* 4.2. As we have seen (pp. 103 ff.), in those sources the word *ma'amad* signified both the representations of the priests, Levites, and Israelites in Jerusalem, and the gathering in the towns of the provincial Israelites who could not go to Jerusalem when the priests and Levites of their *mishmar* went up to serve their ministry in the Temple. The custom of holding these gatherings continued even after the *mishmarot* of the priests and Levites ceased to be identified as regions, but were known as clans. The country still remained divided into regions, each of which celebrated a week in the winter and another in the summer, when it had a special relation to the Temple ritual.

But the ritual of these *ma'amadot* had been fixed in pre-Exilic times. The people gathered to recite by heart passages from the Pentateuch. The yearly cycle of readings from the Pentateuch was interrupted, the Mishna records, for the week of the *ma'amad* (Mishna *Megillah* 3.4).

The early Mishna describing this ritual mentions neither the *Shema'* nor the priestly blessing. Apparently, however, the priestly blessing was introduced into this service at an early time, as is indicated in Mishna *Ta'anit* 4.1. So was the recitation of the *Shema'*. To make sure that everyone attending the service recited the *Shema'*, and assuming some had failed to do so at sunrise, it was added to the *ma'amad* service which was held somewhat later. On Mondays, time had to be allowed for the people to go from their hamlets into the cities. Perhaps some of the men of the *ma'amad* went home each night, and time had to be allowed for their return the next morning. When they did arrive the regular ritual of the *ma'amad, viz.,* the recital of the assigned portion of the day, was observed immediately. The recital of the *Shema'* (and the priestly blessing) followed. Thus the *Shema'* was recited by the men of the *ma'amad* long after sunrise; so that one who joined them in this service did not really fulfill his obligation according to the rule fixing the time of the *Shema'* ritual just before sunrise.

NOTES TO CHAPTER I

1. It is perhaps relevant to this discussion to note that B. Mazar T. Dothan, and I. Dunavesky, in *En Gedi Excavations in June 1962* (p. 6, cf. p. 8 and p. 20) suggest that the midrashic interpretation of Jeremiah 52.16 is of Exilic origin. The verse reads: "But Nebuzaradan, the captain of the guard, left of the poorest of the land to be vinedressers and husbandmen." On this Rab Joseph remarks, citing a *baraita,* "The vinedressers were the gatherers of *apharsamon* from En Gedi to Ramta" (*B. Shabbat* 26a). There is some archaeological support for the view that the production of perfume from the *apharsamon* in En Gedi began with the reign of King Josiah (see *op. cit.* p. 20). It may well be that the source cited by Rab Joseph was transmitted by Babylonian exiles, and was formulated by them many centuries before his time. Professor B. Mazar called my attention to this discovery after this study had been written.

2. The date of the composition of the Judean Scrolls is still being debated. The literature on them is immense and constantly increasing. For the argument that at least some of them were composed before or during the early Maccabean period, see *e.g.* F. R. Cross, *The Ancient Library of Qumran,* pp. 88 ff., and other works cited in the bibliography to this volume.

3. See *Harvard Theological Review,* XXXI, 1938, pp. 291-377; and XXXVI, 1942, pp. 291-332, and XXXVII, 1943, pp. 1-38.

4. The Book of Jubilees is dated in the early part of the Second Century B.C.E. by Eduard Meyer, *Ursprung u. Anfaenge d. Christentums* II, pp. 45 ff.; and W. F. Albright, *From the Stone Age to Christianity,* pp. 266 ff. The usual date given is still the age of John Hyrcan (see R. H. Charles, *Apochrypha and Pseudepigrapha of the O.T.* II, p. 6). Cf., however, *Harvard Theological Review,* XXXVII, pp. 19 ff., where I believe I have demonstrated that the book was written during the period of the struggle between the Hellenists and the traditionalists, just prior to the Maccabean Rebellion.

5. Examples of the use by the author of the Book of Jubilees of midrashic exegesis, found in Rabbinic works of a much later date but obviously of very early origin, are plentiful. A few may be noted here.

(I) Jubilees 30.10 interprets Leviticus 18.21 precisely as does *Targ. Ps. Jonathan* on the verse, R. Ishmael in *Midrash Tannain* 18.9, p. 109 (quoted anonymously in a gloss to *Sifre* Deut. 171, p. 218, but rejected as misleading in Mishna *Megillah* 4.9 ; but *cf.* the comment of Ch. Albeck in his Appendix to his ed. of the Mishna, *Megillah,* p. 505). *Cf.* my discussion of the passage in *Harvard Theological*

Review XVI, 1923, p. 57; and that of Ch. Albeck in *Das Buch d. Jubilæen u. die Halacha*, p. 55.

(II) The author of the Book of Jubilees (7.20) clearly knew the tradition that the sons of Noah had been given six commandments; and apparently was acquainted with the norm listing them. See my discussion of the subject in *Harvard Theological Review, loc. cit.*, p. 60; and *cf. Seder 'Olam R.* Chap. 5, ed. Marx, p. 13; *Tosefta 'Aboda Zara* 8 (9).4, p. 473; *B. Sanhedrin* 56a; *Bereshit R.* Chap. 16.16, ed. Theodor p. 149 (where the commandments are said to have been given to Adam); *Pesiqta d'Rab Kahana* 12.1, ed. Buber, p. 100b, ed. B. Mandelbaum, p. 202; and cross references there given.

(III) *Sifre* Deut., 311, p. 352 interprets the verse, "When the Most High gave to the nations their inheritance, when He separated the children of men, He set the borders of the peoples according to the number of the children of Israel" (Deut. 32.8) as follows: "When the Holy One, blessed be He, caused the world to be inherited by the nations, he defined the boundaries of each nation, so that they should not mix. He sent the children of Gomer to Gomer, the children of Magog to Magog, the children of Madai to Madai, the children of Javan to Javan, the children of Tubal to Tubal; he defined the boundaries of the nations so that they should not come into the Land of Israel."

The Book of Jubilees, apparently drawing on this Midrash, maintains that *Noah* divided the world among his three sons (Jub. 8. 12 ff.), carefully defining the areas of each of his three sons. The central portion of the world was given to Shem and his descendants, the north to Japhet, and the south, i.e. the whole of North Africa up to the Atlantic Ocean, to Ham. But, claims the author, Canaan, the son of Ham, unjustly seized the land called afterward by his name, despite protests of his own father, Ham, and his brothers (Jub. 10.29 ff.).

In this way the author established the historical claim of Israel to the Holy Land, after the manner customary among Hellenistic writers of the period. His theory also explained the origin of Carthage as a Phoenician colony; the Phoenicians being identical with the Canaanites. Possibly, therefore the author was also acquainted with *Mekilta, Bo,* Chap. 18, p. 69, which explains the origin of Carthage on the theory that the Canaanites left the Holy Land in order to make room for the people of Israel. According to *Mekilta,* the land was called Canaan in honour of the graciousness of the Canaanites in leaving the country, and turning it over to the Israelites. (Later *Midrashim* substitute the names of other people, such as the Girgashites, for the Canaanites; see notes of Horovitz to *Mekilta, loc. cit.*).

The author of the Book of Jubilees may have wished to suggest that far from deserving praise for having left the land, Canaan was blameworthy in having entered it. In any event, it seems clear that the Book of Jubilees drew on *Sifre, loc. cit.*

For other examples of the use of early *Midrashim* by the author, *cf.* Ch. Albeck, *op. cit.*; and my own discussion in *Harvard Theological Review, loc. cit.*

6. The most important book on this subject remains Z. Fraenkel, *Ueber d. Einfluss d. palaest. Exegese auf d. alex. Hermeneutik.* But see also J. N. Epstein, *Mebuot le-Sifrut ha-Tannaim,* pp. 516 ff.

7. A. Thus, the Chronicler indicates that the blood of the paschal lamb was dashed against the altar (II Chron. 30.16). This is not commanded anywhere in the Pentateuch; but it is established on the basis of a midrashic interpretation of Deuteronomy 12.27. (See *Meshech Hokmah* by R. Meir Simhah of Dvinsk, *ad loc.,* who indicates that "the Torah of Moses" in Chronicles—as well as, one may add, in other historical Books of the Bible—means not the Pentateuch, but Deuteronomy).

B. In HUCA, XXXII, 1961, Hebrew section, pp. 1 ff., I have shown that the original *baraita* explaining Deut, 17.8 ff. limited the prerogatives of the Temple court as a court of appeal to issues of capital punishment and matters of ritual. Other questions, such as civil controversies, were not necessarily to be referred to the Temple court. Apparently, they were to be referred to the Court of the Proto-Pharisaic Sages of Israel. This interpretation of Deuteronomy 17.8 ff. was apparently accepted also by the Chronicler, who ascribes the view to King Jehoshaphat (II Chron. 19.5 ff.). According to the Chronicler, King Jehoshaphat in his instructions to the Court which he set up in Jerusalem, paraphrased Deuteronomy 17.8 ff., stating that the Court in Jerusalem was to hear cases "between blood and blood" (apparently those involving charges of murder), "between law and commandment, statutes and ordinances." The substitution of these terms, for the Pentateuchal ones "between blood and blood, between plea and plea, between stroke and stroke," was deliberate. The Pentateuchal expression suggested that the Court of Jerusalem was authorised to give final decisions in any controversies among the inhabitants. The Chronicler's version, like that of the Proto-Pharisaic tradition, limited it to cases of murder and ritual matters.

C. Another example of the use of an early *Midrash* by the Chronicler seems to be implied in another part of his discussion of Hezekiah's Passover celebration (II Chron., *loc. cit.*). Professor Saul Lieberman has shown in *Sinai Jubilee Volume,* pp. 80 ff., that the "impurity" of the people which compelled Hezekiah to celebrate the Passover in the second month, was, according to the Chronicler, impurity caused through contact with idolatry, a form of impurity not specifically mentioned in Scripture. This type of impurity was held to be as severe as that caused through affliction with "a flow" (Lev. 15.1 ff.) or through leprosy (*ibid.,* 14.2 ff.). These may be multiplied.

8. See his *Mebuot le-Sifrut ha-Tannaim,* p. 501.

9. B. Jacob, *Im Nammen Gottes,* pp. 16 ff.; also *cf.* H.

Zimmerman, *Elohim*, Berlin, 1900, pp. 64 ff. See also my discussion of the subject of cyphers used for the Tetragrammaton in *Harvard Theological Review*, XXXVI, 1943, p. 296, especially notes 16, 17, and 18, and references there given.

10. See my discussion of the subject in the article mentioned in the preceding note.

11. This form is actually followed in many of the benedictions of the current ritual, except that of course the Tetragrammaton has been replaced with the usual cypher (called in the Talmud *'aleph dalet*, after its first two letters).

12. According to the text of *Yerushalmi,* this custom is heretical.

13. This custom is actually followed in many blessings found in the extant prayerbooks. Thus the blessing for the Sabbath begins, "Our God and God of our fathers, take delight in our rest." Its doxology reads: "Blessed art Thou, O Lord, Who dost sanctify the Sabbath." (In the ritual of the Land of Israel, the concluding words were, "Who dost sanctify Israel and the Sabbath" as is indicated in *Ha-Hilluqim sheben bnai Mizrah ubne Erez Yisrael,* ed. M. Margoliot, p. 85 and references there given). Other examples may be cited from the festival prayers. In the daily prayers, some benedictions begin with an address to "our Father," as in the prayer, "Forgive us, our Father for we have transgressed." The doxology always contains the cypher *'aleph dalet* replacing an original Tetragrammaton. Some prayers, however, omit any form of address to the Deity in the opening strophe, as in the section, "Restore our judges as of old." It seems probable that these benedictions, in which neither the Tetragrammaton nor the cypher *'aleph lamed* were used, were composed after the *baraita* under discussion. The authors of these prayers hesitated to use the Tetragrammaton; but also did not wish to use the cypher *'aleph lamed,* which is deprecated in the *baraita.* Therefore they used another term, or omitted any form of address to the Deity.

14. According to the reading of *Yerushalmi,* this form is that of the totally ignorant.

15. See *Tosefta Kifeshutah, Berakot,* p. 122; *Proceedings of the American Academy for Jewish Research,* XX, pp. 395 ff.

16. This is the reading of Ms. Vienna. That of the citation in the Commentary of Rabbi Samson of Sens on Mishna *Yadaim,* end, is virtually the same. Much of the text is omitted in *ed. pr.* and following it, in all the other eds. of *Tosefta.* Zuckermandel, in his ed. of *Tosefta,* did not take note of the reading of Ms. Vienna. But it has been amply discussed by Professor Saul Lieberman in his *Tosefet Rishonim* IV, p. 160. He notes that the sect of "Morning-Bathers" was mentioned by the Church Fathers, particularly Eusebius. See also the discussion of the subject by Professor Louis Ginzberg in his *Commentary on the Yerushalmi II,* pp. 230 ff.

17. All the texts of *Mekilta* read, "Yesterday you were worshipping *Bel Qores Nebo,*" citing Isaiah 46.1, but surprisingly

taking *qores*, which is a verb meaning "boweth down," and describing the humiliation of the idol *Bel*, as a noun, as though it were the name of a Babylonian god, like *Bel* and *Nebo*. How this misinterpretation occurred is difficult to say. Apparently, the original text simply mentioned *Bel*, and the transmitter, recalling Isaiah 46.1, added the two following words. But this difficulty does not bear on the argument in which we are engaged.

18. The verb used here for "squealing" is the root *nSr* and is apparently the ancient Hebrew equivalent of the Aramaic and Mishnaic Hebrew *n'r*, usually employed to describe asses braying (see Prof. Lieberman, in *Leshonenu XXXII*, 1968, pp. 94 ff.). In *ed. pr.* of *Mekilta*, the word is omitted, apparently because the printer or the copyist of the manuscript he used did not understand it. *Midrash Hakamim* reads *mosesim*; *Pesiqta Zutreta* reads *noshrim*, both words apparently intended to mean "spilling," as though the meat of the pigs were spilling from between the teeth of the *ger*. *Tanhumah* reads *nashuk*, i.e., the meat of the pigs is *bitten* between one's teeth. *Tosefta Baba Mezia* 3.25, p. 378, paraphrases the passage as follows: "If one is a *ger*, and comes to study Torah, one must not say to him, 'See who has come to study Torah! One who consumed carcasses and *terefot*, detestable and swarming animals.'" A similar paraphrase is cited in *B. Mezia*, 58b. All these changes and paraphrases indicate how difficult the later authorities found the reading of *Mekilta*.

19. See below, pp. 77 ff.

20. See below, pp. 72 ff.

21. See Professor Saul Lieberman in *Hellenism in Jewish Palestine*, p. 87. This does not imply any denial that individual scholars may have made private notes of it for their own use (see *ibid.*, p. 84). For an opposing view, and a summary of the earlier discussion of the question when the Mishna was put into writing, see J. N. Epstein, *Mabo le-Nusah ha-Mishnah* pp. 692 ff.

22. J. N. Epstein, *Mebuot le-Sifrut ha-Tannaim*, p. 505.

NOTES ON CHAPTER II

1. Professor Louis Ginzberg in his *Commentary on the Yerushalmi*, IV, p. 58, calls attention to the fact that *Sifre* cites only pre-Exilic Prophets as examples. He says: "It is difficult to believe that it is only accidental that not one of the Prophets who flourished after the destruction of the Temple is mentioned in this text."

The norm is discussed at length by Professor Ginzberg in *Commentary on the Yerushalmi ad loc.*, IV, posthumously edited by D. Weiss, pp. 14 ff.; and by Professor Saul Lieberman in *Tosefta Kifeshutah, Berakot* pp. 47 ff.

2. The term *nebiim ha-rishonim*, "the early Prophets," is used by Zecharaiah (1.4) to signify pre-Exilic ones. The Talmud offers

various identifications of "the early Prophets," but all agree that they were pre-Exilic. According to one view, they were the "earliest Prophets," contemporaries of King David; according to others, the phrase meant contemporaries of Jeremiah (*B. Sotah* 48b; *Yer. ibid.* 9.14, 24b). The term *nebiim 'aharonim,* "the last Prophets" or "the latter Prophets," signifies Haggai, Zechariah, and Malachi (*Yer., loc. cit.; Tosefta Sotah* 13.2, ed. Zuckermandel. p. 318). See discussion by Professor Louis Ginzberg in his *Commentary on the Yerushalmi* IV, pp. 56 ff.

3. The passage is cited in somewhat different form in *B. Berakot* 31a; *Yer. ibid.,* 5.1, 8d.

4. P. 207.

5. See *Vayyikra Rabba* 6.6, ed. Margoliot, p. 142, Professor Saul Lieberman has called attention to a *Midrash* according to which two verses prophesied by Eldad and Medad were added to the Pentateuch! (See his notes to *Vayyikra Rabba,* ed. Margoliot, p. 872). He has also called to my attention his note in the Hebrew translation of *Hellenism in Jewish Palestine* (*Yevanim ve-Yevanut be-Erez Yisrael,* p. 180, n. 28), where he cites *Midrash Mishle* regarding two verses "which were a separate book and were hidden," *i.e.,* became apochryphal.

NOTES ON CHAPTER III

1. *Cf.* above, p 14.

2. In his commentary on *Sifre,* R. Hillel explains that both Books are contained in the present work of Jeremiah; but that the prophecies regarding Babylonia constituted a separate treatise, as Jer. 51.60 states, "And Jeremiah wrote in one book all the evil that should come upon Babylon, even all these words that are written concerning Babylon." This view is certainly possible; but it still suggests an early date for the homilist, in whose time the two parts of the Book of Jeremiah had not yet been united.

3. Conceivably, the purpose of the homilist was to *establish* the canonicity of the Psalter. He demonstrated from II Sam. 23 that King David had uttered other prophecies than that cited there; these prophecies, he may have implied, were the Book of Psalms, or at least one of the Books now constituting the Psalter, or perhaps still uncollected Psalms. Even if that was the purpose of the homilist's remark, it shows that in his day the Psalter's place in the canon was by no means generally accepted; and had to be argued.

4. According to ARN I, Chap. I, 1b, the Book of Proverbs, like the Song of Songs and Koheleth were apochrypha for centuries, "until the Men of the Great Synagogue came and interpreted them." See also ARN II, chap. I, 2a. Various commentators, including Solomon Schechter, have substituted "the men of Hezekiah, King of Judah" for the "Men of the Great Synagogue," but the text can

hardly be emended against all the manuscripts and the first edition. We must assume that the authors held that these works were apochrypha until the time of the Men of the Great Synagogue; that is, they were not accepted into the canon until that time. This tradition seems to be related to that which attempts to include the name of King Solomon among those who, according to Mishna *Sanhedrin,* Chap. 10, have no share in the Future World. A man declared to have forfeited his share in the Future World could hardly be considered author of part of the Sacred Scriptures. (For the discussion of the effort to condemn King Solomon, see *B. Sanhedrin* 104b ; *Yer. ibid.,* 29b). It was the opinion of Rab (that is correct reading, see *Diqduqe Soferim, ad loc.*) that the list of those denied the Future World was made by the Men of the Great Synagogue (*B. Sanhedrin* 104a). I owe these insights to a discussion with Professor Saul Lieberman.

5. See above, p. 14.

6. The reading "Jeremiah" is found in *ed. pr., Yalkut,* and Ms. British Museum. All other texts read, "the Lord," as do the Massoretic text of the Bible itself and all the versions. In my edition of *Sifre* Deut., I followed the majority of the mss., particularly as they agreed with the Massoretic text and the versions. The texts having this reading include those usually most reliable, *viz.* Ms. Vatican and Ms. Berlin. The reading is also found in *Midrash ha-Gadol* and *Pesiqta Zutreta.* Nevertheless, it now seems clear to me that the original reading in *Sifre* was "Jeremiah." The context shows that this must have been the original reading ; for only on the basis of that reading could *Sifre* ask, "Did *Jeremiah* prophesy only these chapters?" The *Sifre* texts which substitute the Massoretic reading for the word "Jeremiah" were "corrected" to agree with it, even though as thus corrected the passage makes no sense. Indeed, because the citation as it stands in the mss. agreeing with the Massoretic text does not make sense, Rashi (Eccl. beg.) quoting *Sifre,* and *Yalkut* (Eccl. beg.) both substitute for the verse cited in *Sifre* the opening verse of Jeremiah. R. Elijah Gaon of Vilna proposed to emend the text of *Sifre* through adding Jer. 30.1, "The word that came to Jeremiah from the Lord saying. . .," and substituting the reading of the Massoretic text for that of *ed. pr.* in the citation of Jer. 30.4.

However, it seems clear that the original reading of *Sifre* was, as observed, "Jeremiah." The fact that *Sifre* preserves a reading not found in the Massoretic Text or any of the versions, itself indicates the extremely early date of the composition. It was composed before the time of the LXX, which already has the altered reading, now found in all the versions.

7. *B. Baba Batra* 14b.

8. *Sifre* Deut. 1.1.

9. *Sifre* Deut. 342, p. 391 ; and *cf.* above, p. 14.

10. The meaning of the word "prophesy" in this homily is by no means clear. It is not certain that the author meant that the Book of Ecclesiastes was a canonical work. He may not even have meant that the "prophecies" of King David, to which he refers, were canonical. Nor did he necessarily mean that the oral traditions going back to Amos, to which he refers, had the status of inspired words. Apparently the homilist used the term "prophecies" in the same sense as the Chronicler in some passages (*cf.* I Chron. 25.1 ff). For him "prophesy" meant "compose sacred works," not necessarily Prophetic works in the traditional sense of the term. In that event, it is possible, although not probable, that the reference to the Book of Ecclesiastes was made by the original homilist.

11. Mishna *Yadaim,* Chap. 3, end.

NOTES ON CHAPTER IV

1. *Cf. Sifre* Deut. 48, p. 108, lines 1 ff.; *ibid.,* p. 113, lines 5 ff.; *Sifra Behuqotai* beg. paragraph 2 ff., 110c. See further below, p. 30.

NOTES ON CHAPTER V

1. *See Seder 'Olam Rabbah* Chap. 3, ed. Ratner 7b, ed. Marx, p. 7; *Yer. Sotah,* Chap. 5, end; *B. Baba Batra* 15a. In ARN I, Chap. 2, 6b, Job is listed immediately after Moses and before the Prophets. In ARN II, Chap. 2, 4b, he is listed before Moses. Authorities, cited in *Yer. Sotah* and *B. Baba Batra, loc. cit.,* maintained that he was an Israelite, and was therefore no exception to the rule set down in *Sifre.*

NOTES ON CHAPTER VI

1. See above, pp. 14, 18, 24.
2. See above, p. 9.
3. The *Midrashim* of the School of R. Akiba, of which *Mekilta of R. Simeon* was one, contain material deriving from the School of Shammai which, in turn, based its views in large part on that of the Temple priests. Thus I have demonstrated that the portion of *Sifre* Deut., emanating from the School of R. Akiba, (*Sifre* on Deut. 12.1-26.15), bears the stamp of Shammaitic scholarship (see *Jubilee Vol. in Honour of Rabbi Simhah Asaf,* pp. 415 ff.). The same influence may be perceived in many passages of *Sifra,* likewise a *midrash* from the School of R. Akiba (see my Introduction to the facsimile ed. of *Sifra, Ms. Assemani* 66, pp. 13, 38, 66. There I also cited one passage in the transmitted text of *Mekilta of R. Simeon* reflecting the influence of R. Eliezer, who so frequently transmitted Shammaitic traditions).

4. The controversy regarding the relative merits of study and observance of ritual continued in Judaism for centuries. It was most clearly articulated at the famous meeting in Lod in which R. Tarfon, R. Akiba and R. José the Galilean participated (*Sifre* Deut. 41, p. 85; *B. Qiddushin* 40b; *Yer. Pesahim* 3.6, 30b; *Shir ha-Shirim R.* 2.14). R. Akiba placed study above observance, but his colleagues placed observance of the Commandments above study. However, it seems evident that the controversy was even more ancient. Simeon the Righteous in his maxim emphasized the primacy of Torah, coming even before the ritual of the Temple, although he was a priest (Mishna *Abot* 1.3). For reference to other texts reflecting this difference of opinion, see my discussions in *Akiba* pp. 49 ff.; as well as in *The Pharisees* I, pp. 96 ff.; and in *Ha-Perushim ve-Anshe Keneset ha-Gedolah* pp. 11 ff.

5. See ARN II Chap. 10, 13b, Solomon Schechter considered the comment there cited as a late gloss, because it startled him to find so clear an expression of the view that fear of God is a motivation in religion superior to love of God. *Cf.* my discussion of the subject in *Mabo le-Mesiktot Abot ve-Abot d'Rabbi Natan.* pp. 32 ff.

6. See below, p. 77 ff.

NOTES ON CHAPTER VII

1. *Sifre* Deut. 310, p. 351.

2. The rendering, "He will grant him understanding," is that implied, as will be seen, in *Sifre*. It is not the rendering of modern translations.

3. Many texts read here "the four kingdoms," referring apparently to Dan. 7.17. But the word "four" is missing in the Berlin Ms. and in *Midrash Hakamim,* which are extremely reliable. Moreover, the tendency of a copyist finding the term "kingdoms" in such a context would be to add the word "four;" because the concept of the four kingdoms pervades the whole Talmudic and Midrashic literature.

4. *Sifre* Deut. 313, p. 356.

5. *Midrash Tannaim,* p. 191.

NOTES ON CHAPTER VIII

1. I have suggested long ago that the synagogue originated in such pre-Exilic Prophetic gatherings (see *Proceedings of the American Academy for Jewish Research,* 1931-32, pp. 49 ff.). This thesis was accepted and defended by Leopold Loew (see his *Gesammelte Schriften* IV, pp. 5 ff.). See also S. Baron, *The Jewish Community* III, p. 9, n. 14. For references to other theories of the origin of the synagogue, see *The Pharisees* II, p. 880, n. 18.

Synagogues, as structures, did not exist in very early times. In Jerusalem during the Second Commonwealth prayer was generally offered under the open sky, just as study was offered in the open. ARN II, Chap. 27, 28a, describes a scene wherein people are praying in the Temple courts. From the context it seems clear that these prayers were the formal ones. See below, p. 93. Even now, it is customary to hold regular service before the Western Wall in Jerusalem. Such gatherings would have been called "synagogues" in ancient times. See also *The Pharisees*, p. 432.

2. The changes in the synagogue liturgy caused by the persecutions of Antiochus have not as yet been adequately studied. However, one change introduced during that period can be readily documented—the Proclamation of the *Shema'*, as a public ceremony before the recital of the *'amidah*. From Mishna *Tamid* 5.1, ed. A. Brody, p. 76, it is evident that this ceremony was performed as part of the Temple ritual, at least in the final decades of the Second Commonwealth. The service there described makes no reference to the *'amidah*. The Mishna asserts that the priests recited only one blessing before the *Shema'*; a second after it, *viz.* that which in the present synagogue service still follows it. Then they said *Hodaah* (regarding which see below, p. 126) and recited the Priestly Blessing. This service could not have been taken over from the synagogue. Had it been, we should have expected it to include some part of the *'amidah*, as well as the reading of the Torah on Mondays, Thursdays, Sabbaths, festivals, and fast days. One must therefore take it for granted that this ritual *originated* in the Temple.

Every Jew was required to recite the *Shema'* in the early morning (Mishna *Berakot* i.2 f.) as well as at night, whether or not he participated in the synagogue service. Indeed, Mishna *Berakot*, Chap. I, discusses the recital of the *Shema'* as though the usual custom were to perform the ritual privately. Nevertheless, we know from Mishna *Megillah* 4.3 ff., that the *Shema'* was "proclaimed" in the synagogue service. (For the meaning of *pores et Shema'* as "proclamation of the *Shema'*," see my discussion of the term in JQR, N.S. XXXII (1941-42), pp. 387 ff., XXXIII (1942-43), pp. 29 ff.).

When was this custom introduced into the synagogue? Light is shed on this question by *Tosefta Berakot* 1.2., ed. Lieberman p. 1, which reads: "The proper time for it [*i.e.,* for recital of the *Shema'*] is the sunrise, in order to recite the prayer immediately *after it*." (In Ms. Erfurt and in *ed. pr.* this reading has been altered to read, "in order to pray immediately *after the blessing for the redemption*." According to all extant rituals, this blessing follows the *Shema'*. That variant reading, however, was made to reconcile the statement of *Tosefta* with B. *Berakot* 9b, which specifically states that the purpose of reading the *Shema'* at sunrise was to "recite the prayer immediately after the blessing for the redemption." According to the correct reading, *Yer. Berakot* 1.5, 3a, like *Tosefta*, states that the purpose of reciting the *Shema'* at sunrise was that "prayer should be recited immediately after *it*." That reading, too, has been altered in all texts, except the Genizah manuscripts, to conform to the statement of Babli: See Professor Louis Ginzberg, *Commentary on Yerushalmi* I, p. 119, and Professor Saul Lieberman, *Tosefta Kifeshutah, Berakot* p. 2).

The statement that one read the *Shema'* at sunrise so that one could say the prayers immediately *after it,* surely was composed when the *Shema'* was not yet followed by the blessing for the redemption. But this blessing is an integral part of the ceremony of the Proclamation of the *Shema',* as shown by Mishna *Tamid, loc. cit.* (It is difficult to accept the view that the norm is formulated to apply to the exceptional instances of persons who, defiled because of cohabitation with their wives and not yet bathed, were forbidden to say the blessings of the *Shema'*). There was, therefore, a time when the blessings of the *Shema',* and indeed the ritual of the Proclamation of the *Shema',* were unknown in the synagogue service. The ritual was added to the synagogue service from the Temple service.

The change was made long before the Hadrianic persecutions. At that time, the blessings—originally said only at a public service as part of the Proclamation of the *Shema'*—were added in the ritual of the private reading of the *Shema',* as described in Mishna *Berakot* 1.2 ff. Before the Hadrianic persecutions, the blessings before and after the *Shema'* were said only at public services. This is evident from Mishna *Megillah* 4.6, where R. Judah states that a person born blind must not proclaim the *Shema'* (apparently because he cannot recite the first blessing *viz.,* that for light, never having experienced it). R. Judah does not say that a blind person should not recite this blessing in his private performance of the ritual of the *Shema'.* The reason for his limiting the norm to the public proclamation of the *Shema'* must be that the blessing for the light was not said otherwise than at a public service.

In view of the fact that the ceremony of the Proclamation of the *Shema'* was in existence before the Hadrianic persecutions, it seems highly probable that it was introduced into the synagogue service at the time of the great persecution preceding that of Hadrian, namely, that of Antiochus IV.

Because of the defilement of the Temple, and the impossibility of performing the ritual of the Proclamation of the *Shema'* there, it was transferred to the synagogue prayer gatherings. Because this ritual was, in origin, taken over from the Temple, an early Mishna takes it for granted that a priest would preside over it exactly as in the Temple custom (Mishna *Megillah* 4.5 ; see the discussions of the text in the Talmud and by the commentators; and especially in the discussion by Ch. Albeck, in his *Additions and Appendices* to his ed. of the Mishna II, p. 503).

The difficulty of the commentators in explaining that Mishna shows that it reflects conditions of a time when the ritual was different than that of later generations. The ceremony of the Proclamation of the *Shema'* was apparently adopted in all synagogues, after it had been introduced into the synagogue ritual by priests who remembered it from the Temple ceremony.

3. See preceding note; and see also *Akiba*, pp. 252 ff. The custom of sounding the *shofar* on Rosh ha-Shanah as a ritual separate from the recital of the *'amidah*, apparently goes back to the persecutions of Hadrian. The people could not sound the *shofar* during the regular service, when Roman soldiers watched them. They therefore had to sound the *shofar* after the soldiers left. See Professor Saul Lieberman, *Tosefta Kifeshutah, Berakot* p. 41; and his references there. He shows that in the time of the Schools of Hillel and Shammai, the *shofar* was sounded at the *shaharit* service, rather than, as now, at the *musaf* service on *Rosh ha-Shanah*. The change from the morning service to the later service was doubtless due to the Hadrianic persecutions.

4. For the meaning of *Ribbebot Qodesh*, cf. *Sifre, ad loc*. According to some interpretations preserved there, the phrase refers to the hosts of angels (*cf. ibid.*, p. 398). However, other passages in *Sifre* apparently take the phrase to mean a region (*cf. ibid.*, p. 395, line 13.)

5. The reading "hired" is found only in *ed. pr.* where it is followed by the letters *lamed aleph*. However, these are simply the first letters of the following word. In Ms. Br. Mus. (which is derived from the same group as *ed. pr.*; see *Proceedings of the American Academy for Jewish Research*, 1931-1932, p. 10) the reading is *v-nizrak*, not *v-nidrak*, as indicated in my edition. However, *v-nizrak* may be a corruption for *v-nidrak*, meaning "to be authorized," see Professor Saul Lieberman in J.Q.R., N.S., XXXV, 1944, p. 27. The other texts read *v-nizkar*, "and he was remembered." This may be a corruption of *v-nizrak—v-nidrak*.

6. This is the reading of *Yalkut*, Ms. Br. Mus., *Genizah*, and *ed. pr. Midrash Tannaim* reads, similarly, "by one to speak for him." Ms. Berlin and *Midrash Hakamim* have an emended reading, "to speak in the interests of a particular person."

7. An alternative reading may be *'oleh* ("he who goes up"), referring to the *rhetor* himself, ("Happy is he who may come before the judge, or the king, to speak on behalf of someone"). This reading is found in Ms. Br. Mus. and *Yalkut*. The copyist who wrote *'oleh* for *'olam* was doubtless troubled by the use of the word *'olam* "world" without the article "the" (*i.e. ha'olam*), which would be far more natural. But the ancient homilist was apparently translating literally the Latin used in the acclamation of the Emperor. As the Latin has no "the," he rendered the acclamation, "Happy is world because of its King." See Professor Saul Lieberman in J.Q.R., N.S., XXXV, 1944, p. 27.

8. The reading of all the texts except *Midrash Tannaim* is *mimalko*, which might be taken to mean "because of its king."

However, *mimalko* is simply a contraction of the two words, *mi malko,* meaning "considering who is its king." This is shown by the corresponding reading of *Midrash Tannaim,* which is *mi betoko,* "considering who is in it." The contraction of *mi malko* into one word *mimalko* follows the common use of Palestinian sources, *cf.* the similar spelling of two such words as one in the Mishna, see J. N. Epstein, *Mabo le-Nusah ha-Mishnah* p. 1218, and apparently even in Scripture, *cf.* Num. 23.10, *u-mispar,* which should be rendered as though it were written *umi safar,* "and who has counted."

9. See note 7.

10. The reading, *mi dayyano* (as two words), meaning "considering who is his judge," is found in *Midrash Tannaim.* In *Midrash Hakamim, Yalkut,* and *Genizah,* the ancient spelling as one word, *midayyano,* has been retained. Ms. Berlin reads *mimanhigo,* "because of its leader," or better, "considering who is its leader." The texts of Br. Mus. and *ed. pr.* have been corrupted. See note 8.

11. This is the reading of *Yalkut, ed. pr.,* and *Genizah.* Ms. Berlin and *Midrash Hakamim* read, *"And others* joined him in hailing the King." The phrase is omitted in *Midrash Tannaim.*

12. *Midrash Tannaim, Yalkut,* and *ed. pr.* read, "to the needs."

13. The word "benedictions" is omitted in *Yalkut,* Ms. Br. Mus., and *ed. pr.*

14. The reading, "the early Prophets" is found only in Ms. Berlin and *Midrash Hakamim. Yalkut,* Ms. Br. Mus., *Genizah,* and *ed. pr.* read *hakamim,* "Sages." *Midrash Tannaim* reads "Sages and Prophets." See discussion below, p. 44.

Midrash Tehillim 17.4 (ed. Buber, 64a) undoubtedly drawing on *Sifre* states, "Therefore the early *hasidim* ("saints") ordained that three prayers be recited each day." The editor or transmitter has replaced the word "Prophets" with "saints," because of the tradition that the prayers were composed by the authorities of post-Prophetic times. (This is the only reading given by Buber in his edition, and is that of edds. Constantinople 1512, and Venice 1546. Professor Shmuel Leiter has kindly let me have the variant readings from the various mss., most of which have the same reading as edds. Constantinople and Venice. However, Ms. Florence 13, Bibliotheca Laurenziana Pl. Z. 13, and Ms. Trinity Loewe 48, read "Sages" (*hakamim*) instead of *hasidim.* Ms. Or. 786 of the University Library in Cambridge has *hakamim.* But dots have been placed over the letters and *hasidim* written afterward). However, the same passage occurs in *Midrash Shemuel* 31.4, (ed. Buber p. 138); and there the reading is, precisely as in the texts of *Sifre* cited here, "Therefore the early *Prophets* ordained that the people of Israel should pray thrice each day." The citation in *Midrash Shemuel* offers further evidence, if any were needed, that the reading "Prophets" in *Sifre* is authentic.

15. Ms. Berlin and *Midrash Hakamim* add "every day," a reading which I adopted in my edition of *Sifre.* However, the words

are missing in *Yalkut*, Ms. Br. Mus., *Genizah*, and *ed. pr.*, and may be an editorial addition. *Midrash Tannaim* omits the phrase, "that Israel should pray."

16. The words "Holy art Thou and awesome is Thy Name," are added here in *Yalkut*, *Genizah* Ms., and *ed. pr.*; and I followed them in my edition. Ms. Br. Mus., the source which doubtless had the same reading, now has (through a copyist's error) "Holy and awesome is Thy Name." But the words are missing in Ms. Berlin and in *Midrash Hakamim*; and seem to have been added to the parent text of French-German Mss. from a marginal gloss (see *Preceedings of the Amer. Acad. for Jewish Research, loc. cit.*). For the reading of *M* see below, p. 43.

17. The reading given in the text follows that of *Yalkut*, Ms. Br. Mus., and *ed. pr.* *Genizah* reads "and after that, 'Who releasest the captives,'" etc. Ms. Berlin, deriving from a "corrected" text, the copyist of which assumed that *Sifre* referred to the Babylonian version of the second benediction of the *'amidah*, which reads "Who healest the sick, releasest the captives," gives the attributes in that order.

18. This is the reading of Ms. Berlin which, because of its difficulty and oddity, must be accepted as probably original. *Midrash Hakamim* reads, "and we acknowledge Thee," citing the first words of the customary benediction of *Modim*. *Yalkut*, Ms. Br. Mus., and *ed. pr.*, the reading of which I adopted in my edition have "and after that, 'We acknowledge Thee.'"

19. See Professor Saul Lieberman in *Zalman Schocken Jubilee Volume (Ale Ayyin)* pp. 75 ff.

20. The prayer beginning *modim 'anahnu lak*, now recited in all synagogue services, is called *hodaah* in various passages of the Mishna, such as *Rosh ha-Shanah* 4.5.

21. The *'amidah* according to that text concludes with the direction of the leader, "And at the end he says, 'And now our God, we acknowledge [or 'prostrate ourselves before'] Thee.'" This version of the ritual is found in no other text. Clearly, from its use of the cypher *'aleph lamed*, the text was compo^ced when the Tetragrammaton was no longer freely pronounced. The composer of this text did not understand *Sifre* to refer to a blessing beginning with *modim 'anahnu lak*. If he had, he would simply have said, "and after that, *'modim 'anahnu lak.'*"

22. For the significance of the root *ydh* as meaning prostration see Professor Saul Lieberman, *Tosefta Kifetushah, Sheqalim* p. 696; and Professor Louis Ginzberg, *Commentary on the Yerushalmi* I, p. 181.

23. Regarding the custom of prostration after the *'amidah*, see Professor Louis Ginzberg, *Ginze Schechter* II, p. 4, and the responsum of Rab Amram Gaon, *ibid.*, p. 19, as well as the parallel passages cited by Professor Ginzberg (*op. cit.*, p. 4). From this responsum, it is clear that even as late as the time of Rab Amram Gaon it was

customary to prostrate oneself after the *'amidah,* and that the custom of putting one's head over one's hand after the *'amidah* was introduced to Babylonia only in late Gaonic periods. Significantly, this later ritual is still called, "falling on one's face." Doubtless, the custom of prostration after the *'amidah* had been followed in earlier times also in the Holy Land. Possibly it was abandoned, as Professor Ginzberg suggests, when the Christians adopted the system of prostrations. See further, Professor Ginzberg's discussion of the subject in *Commentary on the Yerushalmi* I, pp. 182 ff.; III, pp. 116 ff. When the benediction, *hodaah,* and the ceremony of the priestly blessing were added to the *'amidah,* the ritual of prostration necessarily was postponed until they were completed. Therefore, bowing at the beginning and at the end of *hodaah* was substituted for prostration. This custom is recorded in *Tosefta Berakot* 1.8, ed. Lieberman, p. 3; *Yer. Berakot* 1.5.3 c., and in *B. Berakot* 34a. However in Babylonia the custom of prostration at the end of the *'amidah* also persisted, as indicated above.

24. *Abodah* is the name used for the prayer for the Preservation or the Restoration of the Divine Worship in Jerusalem. It was the sixteenth benediction of the daily *'amidah* customary in the land of Israel in rabbinic times; and the seventeenth in that of Babylonia. It is mentioned several times in the Mishna, *cf.* Mishna *Rosh ha-Shanah.* 4.5.

25. See above note 20.

26. *Sifre* Deut., 342, p. 391.

27. R. H. Charles, *Apochrypha and Pseudepigraphs of the O.T.* I, pp. 476 ff.

28. In Ms. Berlin and *Midrash Hakamim* the order is "corrected." But clearly the reading of the other text is, in this instance, the original one.

29. The view that the future redemption must come from God Himself, and cannot come through man, is reflected in the Passover *Haggadah,* which stresses the fact that the redemption from Egypt occurred through the Divine act, and not through an intermediary.

30. *Cf.* J.Q.R., N.S., XVI, 1925, p. 163.

31. *J.Q.R., loc. cit.,* and references given there.

NOTES ON CHAPTER IX

1. I follow the reading of the Mishna, ed. Lowe, the Mishna contained in *Yerushalmi,* and the best codices; see *Ta'anit,* ed. H. Malter, p. 120; and J. N. Epstein, *Mabo le-Nusah ha-Mishnah,* p. 1131. In none of the authoritative texts of the Mishna is the norm explicitly associated with the verse quoted. The words, "Because Scripture says," with which the Mishna opens according to some texts, are not found in these codices. The words were added in

the text used in the Babylonian Talmud, before the quotation of the verse, in order to connect it with the following statement of the Mishna. See J. N. Epstein, *op. cit.* It is therefore probable that the document included in the Mishna originally began simply with the words, "How can a sacrifice be offered in the absence of the donor?" This passage may have been associated with various norms dealing with the sacrificial service.

After the words, "The Israelites gathered in their cities and recited the story of Creation," the current edds. of the Mishna and the Babylonian Talmud contain the following insertion: "The men of the representation fasted four days in the week, from Monday through Thursday. But they did not fast on Friday, out of respect for the Sabbath; nor on Sunday, so that they might not go out from rest and enjoyment into weariness and fasting, and die." The passage, cited in *Yer. ad loc.*, as a *baraita,* is lacking in all the mss. and early edds. of the Mishna.

2. For the meaning of the expression, "the early Prophets," see above, p. 14. As noted in the text, according to *Tosefta Ta'anit* 3(4)2, ed. Lieberman p. 337, an alternative reading of the Mishna was "the Prophets of Jerusalem." There, *Tosefta,* after describing the establishment of the priestly and Levitical clans by Moses and their reorganization by David and Samuel the Seer, states that there "arose *the Prophets of Jerusalem* and established twenty-four representations, corresponding to the twenty-four *mishmarot* of the priesthood and Levitehood." The establishment of twenty-four representations of priests and Levites in Jerusalem to correspond to the twenty-four *mishmarot* would scarcely be logical, unless the *mishmarot* were regions, as is assumed in Mishna *Ta'anit* 4.2. It seems probable, therefore, that the Mishna on which this passage of *Tosefta* is based, read "Prophets of Jerusalem" instead of "the early Prophets." (See below, p. 59).

3. *Mishmar* means literally, "watch." Each region was responsible as a "watch" for the Temple service during the period of its assignment.

4. For a discussion of the various meanings attaching to the term *ma'amad* at different times, see *Appendix C* to this chapter, below pp. 00 ff.

5. *Cf.* comments of H. Malter, *ad loc.*; of R. Solomon Adeni in *Meleket Shelomoh, ad loc.*; Ch. Albeck in his *Additions and Appendices to Mishna Ta'anit,* in his edition of the Mishna, II, pp. 495 ff., and the authorities cited by them.

6. See Mishna *Sheqalim* 4.1, and numerous other passages related to it.

7. *Sifre* Numbers 142, p. 188, does indeed require priests, Levites, and Israelites to be present at the public sacrifices. But in this requirement *Sifre* does not hold that everyone must be present when his own sacrifice is offered. Far from applying such a principle to private sacrifices, *Sifre* cites as the source for the rule a specific

expression on Num. 28.2, dealing only with public sacrifices. For a discussion of the halakic issue involved see *Appendix A* of this chapter.

8. See Mishna *Baba Qamma* 9.12: *Vayyikra* R. 28.2, ed. Margoliot, p. 653 (and notes of Professor Saul Lieberman there, p. 879). The same order was followed by the Qumran sect as is evident from one of its scrolls, in which the order of the festivals is given, each being fixed by the term of the ministry of a particular priestly clan. Thus "The Day of Remembrance," *i.e.* Rosh ha-Shanah, occurred, according to that calendar, during the ministry of the clan Maoziah, which according to I Chron. 24.7 ff. is at the end of the list. Maoziah is followed by Jehoiarib, during whose term of ministry the Day of Atonement occurred. Jehoiarib is followed by Jedaiah, during whose ministry Sukkot occured. The arrangement in the spring was similar. Passover began during the term and ministry of Maoziah; the seventh day occurred during the term of the ministry of Jehoiarib; and that clan was followed by Jedaiah, during the term of whose ministry the *Omer* was sacrificed (see S. Talmon in *Mehqarim bi-megillot ha-Genuzot*, p. 85).

The order listing Jehoiarib first and Jedaiah second is recorded also for the post-Talmudic period. This is true, *e.g.*, in the *Qinah* of R. Eleazar ha-Qalir, still recited on the ninth of Ab. See ed. Abraham Rosenfeld, London, 1965, p. 99; *cf.* S. Klein, *Ma'amarim Shonim la-Haqirat Erez Yisrael*, Section II, pp. 1-24; *Neue Beitraege z. Gesch. u. Geog. Galiläas*, p. 42; P. Kahle, *Masoreten d. Westens,* Hebrew section pp. 1 ff.; M. Zulay, in *Yediot ha-Makon le-Shirah ha-Ibrit bi-Yerushalayim*, V, pp. 113 ff.; S. Abramson in *Tarbiz*, XV, 1944, pp. 51 ff.; E. Fleischer in *Sinai* LXI, 1966-67, pp. 30 ff.; and LXI, 1967-68, pp. 142 ff., and Professor Saul Lieberman in *Tosefta Kifeshutah, Ta'anit*, pp. 1076 ff. For a discussion of the passages in Nehemiah and Chronicles, the variant readings, and the literature on the subject in addition to that cited here, see also E. Schuerer, *Gesch, d. Volkes Israel*, fourth ed., pp. 286 ff., and literature there cited and *cf.* the material in *Appendix C* to this chapter below, p. 102.

9. See above, p. 15.

10. David is apparently counted as a Prophet also in *Mekilta Bo*, Chap. 1, p. 4. See further Introduction of Maimonides to his Code, and the commentary *Abodat ha-Melek* on that passage in the Code. The view that David was a Prophet is mentioned also in the Qumran scrolls; see J. A. Sanders, *The Psalm Scroll of Cave II*, p. 48, line 11.

11. *Tosefta Sotah* 13.5, p. 319; *Yer. ibid.,* 9.14, 24b; *B. ibid.* 33a. See also the expression priest-prophet in *Sifra* Num. 131, line 11 (ed. pr. and some mss. read *high priests*) p. 173, according to the ms. readings cited by H. S. Horovitz in his footnotes. The same expression occurs in Ms. Vatican of *Sifre* Num. 78, p. 74, line 2. The other mss. and *ed. pr.* have other readings.

12. According to *B. Arakin* 12b, the clan of Jehoiarib never returned. However, that opinion is opposed in the Palestinian sources,

according to whose tradition, as shown above, the clan of Jehoiarib did return, and was given the first week in Nisan for its ministry (see Professor Saul Lieberman, *Tosefta Kifeshutah, Ta'anit* p. 1076).
13. See I Chron. 24.7 ff. For Talmudic times, see Mishna *Baba Qamma* 9.12, which implies that the clan of Jedaiah served immediately after that of Jehoiarib. See also literature cited above, note 8.
14. See E. Kaufmann, *Toledot ha-Emunah ha-Yisraelit* VIII, pp. 359 ff.; and article *Kehunah* in *Enzyklopedia Miqrait*.
15. To be sure, Jehoiarib precedes Jedaiah in Neh. 12.6 and 19. But, as noted on p. 102, the Jedaiah of those verses was not the main family of the clan, which is called in that list *Seraiah,* as it is among the signers of the Great Document in Neh. Chap. 10. Apparently, the Qumran Sect also considered it presumptuous that the clan of Jehoiarib should be the first of all. Therefore, in their calendar they began the list with what was in Rabbinic lists the last one, Maoziah (see above n. 8). In their resentment against the Hasmoneans, they rejected the doctrine of Jehoiarib was the first clan, (The title "first of the *mishmarot*" is actually bestowed on the clan of Jehoiarib in *B. Arakin* 13a). In the tradition received by Ben Zoma, and discussed below, p. 65, Jedaiah apparently remained the first of the clans.
16. There is curiously enough no clear record of the order in which the clans ministered in the winter months. The twenty-four clans, mentioned in I Chron. Chap. 24, and in all later records, began their service on the first Sabbath in Nisan, as indicated in the text. What happened when the twenty-four families had all completed their service is not made clear. According to Maimonides, *Hilkot Kle ha-Miqdash* 4.3, the rotation of the clans began again, with Jehoiarib first, Jedaiah second, etc. Thus the twenty-four clans, each serving one more week, would minister at the Temple for altogether forty-eight weeks, beginning with the first Sabbath in Nisan. But how were the other weeks of the year provided for? There seems to be no clarity about this. The text of Maimonides seems to ignore the fact that Jehoiarib always served during the first full week of Nisan, entering on its service with the first Sabbath of that month. Presumably then, Maimonides held that there was no such rule. See *Appendix D* to this chapter for the rule assumed in one record regarding the priestly clans, and which was apparently in force in the last years of the Temple. According to that arrangement, the rule making Jehoiarib the first clan to serve in Nisan was abolished.

Professor Saul Lieberman generously called my attention to the commentary on Chronicles of "The Disciples of Rab Saadia Gaon" (ed. by R. Kirchheim, Frankfort-am-M. 1874), pp. 36 ff. (on I Chron. 23.2), the authors of which apparently held that priestly and Levitical clans served each one week in the winter and one in the summer; and that the remaining weeks of the year belonged to all the priests together. It is difficult to reconcile this view with that of the Mishna, according to which all the clans shared only certain emoluments during the festival weeks, but by no means all, as indicated in the text.

17. *Tosefta Sukkah* 4.19, ed. Lieberman, p. 277.

18. See below, *Appendix B* to this chapter, p. 101.

19. The family of Seorim was apparently a subdivision of one of the four clans which returned under Zerubabel. Of which clan it was a subdivision ; and why it came immediately after Harim is unknown.

20. See above note 16.

21. That the *musaf* prayer originated only after the destruction of the Temple seems clear from various data.

(a) According to Mishna *Berakot* 4.7, R. Eleazar b. Azariah held that the *musaf* prayer could not be recited at all by private individuals, and apparently not even in ordinary synagogues, but only in the assemblage of a city, at a town-meeting as it were. R. Judah offers a variant tradition, according to which individuals did not recite the *musaf* prayer in cities, which had such town-gatherings. But even this tradition—possibly influenced by the conditions which developed during the Hadrianic persecutions—regards the *musaf* prayer as different in character from the others.

(b) R. Joshua b. Hananya describing the activities of those gathered at the Temple during the *Sukkah* week, says: "During the days of the *Sukkah* celebration, we had no sleep. We would awaken to witness the morning sacrifice. From there we would go to the synagogue (i.e. for the morning prayers). From there to witness the *musaf* sacrifice. From there to eat and drink. From there to the house of study. From there to the afternoon sacrifice. From there to the celebration." (*Tosefta Sukkah* 4.5, ed. Lieberman p. 273). This is the reading of ed. pr., Ms. London, and Ms. Vienna. It is significant that that Ms. Erfurt adds, after the reference to the *musaf* sacrifice, "from there to the *musaf* prayers." The copyist noted the omission of any reference to these prayers and, following the text of *B. Sukkah* 53a added it. *Yer. ibid.* 5.2, 55b, however, has the same reading as most texts of *Tosefta,* omitting any reference to the *musaf* prayers. It is difficult to assume that the *musaf* prayers were recited before the *musaf* sacrifices. And indeed the transmitters of the Babylonian version obviously rejected this assumption, and for that reason inserted a specific reference to the *musaf* prayers.

(c) Mishna *Rosh ha-Shanah* 4.5 enumerates nine benedictions for the prayers of *Rosh ha-Shanah.* But it is obvious that the additional benedictions, *Zikronot* and *Shoferot* were recited only at one service. In the extant rituals, this is the *musaf* service. But, as Professor Saul Lieberman has shown (*Tosefta Kifeshutah, Berakot* p. 41), the controversy between the Schools of Shammai and Hillel regarding the recital of these benedictions when *Rosh ha-Shanah* occurs on the Sabbath, applied only to the morning *'amidah.* Indeed, as he observes, this is explicitly asserted in *Yer. Shebuot* 1.5, 33a. But if at the time of the controversy between the schools, the additional benedictions were said only at the morning service, the clear implication of Mishna *Rosh ha-Shanah* 4.5, listing the benedictions of *Rosh ha-Shanah*, and including the additional benedictions, must be that there was only one service—that of the morning—on that day. If the additional benedictions were recited only at one particular service, and omitted at other services, one would expect to find some reference to this distinction. Thus it seems to follow that at the time of the controversy, not only the *musaf* service, but the afternoon service, too, had yet been invented. That fact can be demonstrated from other passages, too; but the discussion would take us too far afield. Suffice it to say here, that it is clear that the *musaf* service was unknown until after the destruction of the Temple, when it was introduced in recollection of the *musaf* sacrifices.

22. The term used in Mishna and *Tosefta* for afternoon is *minhah*. However, this term does not mean the *minhah* service. The word was used regularly as the designation of time, and apparently derived from the fact that at the pre-exilic provincial altars, a meal-offering was sacrificed during the afternoon. Thus Mishna *Shabbat* (1.2) states: "One must not sit down to have one's hair cut about the *minhah* unless one has already prayed." The commentators explain that *minhah* in this passage means the "Time of the *minhah* prayer," but that leaves open the question why the *minhah* prayer should be so called. Moreover, the Babylonian Talmud draws a distinction between the "great *minhah*" and the "small *minhah*," the former being soon after midday, the latter about three hours later. (Cf. e.g. *B. Shabbat* 9b). The commentators and lexicographers have found great difficulty in explaining these terms of the Babylonian Talmud. However, in I Kings 18.29, 36, the time "of the *minhah*", obviously that of the afternoon *minhah*, is used to designate a specific hour. Probably, in provincial sanctuaries, where it was not possible to offer animal sacrifices each day, a large meal offering was sacrificed about noon, and a smaller one in the afternoon. In larger sanctuaries, a lamb would be offered in the morning, and a meal offering in the afternoon. Hence, the time of the meal offering (*minhah*) came to have a specific meaning. The distinction between the large meal offerings of noon time, and the smaller ones of the afternoon is reflected in the Babylonian Talmud's reference to two different times, one of which was called *minhah gedolah*, the other *minhah qetanah*.

23. For the discussion of another norm pointing to the early origin of the *ma'amadot*, see *Appendix E* to this Chapter, p. 110.

NOTES ON CHAPTER X

1. The word "Torah" is frequently employed in the sense of "the Torah." However, there is no evidence that it always has this meaning. Doubtless, at least in some passages, it has the same meaning as in Haggai 2.11, *viz.*, "teaching." The meaning of the opening passage in ARN, and in the Mishna underlying it, may very well be

that Moses received "instruction," *i.e., oral* instruction, from Sinai. This is rendered highly probable by the fact that R. José the Galilean, who commenting on this passage in ARN, added that the instruction was received after the Revelation, also held that the Pentateuch itself was revealed in three places: in Egypt, on Mount Sinai, and in the Tent of Meeting (*Sifra Nedaba* 2.4, 3d). He must, therefore, have interpreted the word "Torah" in the original passage of ARN to mean simply "instruction."

2. I have discussed the nature of this document at length in *Mabo l'-Mesiktot Abot ve-Abot d'Rabbi Natan,* pp. 6 ff. I am repeating it here in order to sharpen one or two points; and for the convenience of the reader.

3. As indicated in the study cited in note 2, the Book of Chronicles enumerates fourteen generations from Aaron to Azariah, the first High Priest (according to the Chronicler) who ministered in the Solomonic Temple (I Chron. 5.36). There were fourteen more generations of High Priests from Azariah to Jaddua, the last High Priest mentioned in Scripture (Neh. 12.11); a contemporary of Alexander the Great, with whom a new era is apparently supposed to begin. The importance attaching to the number fourteen, as a result of the record of the High Priests and of the Pharisaic tradition, may be seen from the emphasis of Matt. 1.17 on the claim that there were fourteen generations from Abraham to David; fourteen from David to the Babylonian Exile; and fourteen more from the beginning of the Exile until Jesus. The author of Matthew probably knew the Mishna in an older form, according to which the fourteen links in the chain of tradition from Moses culminated in Shammai and Hillel (see below). The tradition, according to which great significance attached to the number of links (in the high priesthood) in genealogical descent, was known to the author of the Book of Jubilees, who found it important to record that there were twenty-two generations from Adam to Jacob corresponding to the twenty-two acts of Creation (Jub. 2.23) and to the twenty-two letters of the Hebrew alphabet. The emphasis on the twenty-two acts of Creation as giving importance to the twenty-second generation after Adam, suggests that the author was contravening the tradition of the seven genealogical links corresponding to the seven days of Creation. Perhaps it was in opposition to the teaching of the Book of Jubilees, that Mishna *Abot* 5.1 maintained that the world was created through ten commands; and that these corresponded to the ten generations from Adam to Noah; and the ten generations from Noah to Abraham.

The curious and obscure reference to seven jubilees of different priesthoods in *Test. Levi,* Chap. 17, may be associated with the seven ages predicted in the passage of Mishna *Abot* and ARN under consideration. The purpose of the author may have been to suggest that only the first two "priesthoods," or ages, were periods of righteousness. But this is quite hypothetical.

Anyone inclined to underestimate the significance attaching to

133

such parallelisms in the human mind may do well to consider modern parallels to these arguments which seem so remote from reality or logic. For example, so sophisticated a scientist as Sigmund Freud is said to have been particularly interested in the character and career of Woodrow Wilson, because the latter happened to be born in the same year as he (1856).

4. The belief that the seventh millennium would be that of the Messianic Age or of the Future World occurs frequently (see Professor Louis Ginzberg, *Legends of the Jews* V, p. 128, n. 140, and the many references there cited from midrashic and early Christian sources).

5. Lev. 15.13.

6. *Ibid.*, v. 28.

7. *Ibid.*, v. 19.

8. Num. 19.11.

9. ARN II derives this number from Gen. 50.10.

10. ARN II derives this from Gen. 29.27.

11. See below, pp. 11, 12, where it is shown that according to one version of the early Mishna, Hillel and Shammai constituted the fourteenth link in the chain of tradition. See also above, note 3.

12. According to Mishna *Abot* 2.8, Rabban Johanan ben Zakkai received the tradition from Hillel and Shammai. It seems clear that the authors of the document recording this fact, as well as the maxims of Rabban Johanan ben Zakkai and his five most distinguished disciples, were members of his own School. The compilers of this document did not yet have in the text of their Mishna *Abot* any quotation from Rabban Gamaliel I or Rabban Simeon ben Gamaliel I. Therefore, they associated their compilation directly with the older Mishna, which traced the transmission of the tradition to Hillel and Shammai (see my *Introduction to the Treatises Abot and ARN*, pp. 41 ff.). R. Eliezer is cited in *Tosefta Yadaim* 2.16 (ed. Zuckermandel, p. 683), as claiming that a tradition of his derived from Rabban Johanan ben Zakkai, who had received it "from the Pairs, and the Pairs from the Prophets, and the Prophets from Moses, as a tradition of Moses from Mount Sinai." Significantly, this association of Rabban Johanan ben Zakkai with "the Pairs" was expunged from the corresponding passage in the Mishna (*Yadaim* 4.3), presumably by R. Judah the Patriarch. The Mishna simply states that according to R. Eliezer, Rabban Johanan ben Zakkai had received this tradition from his teacher, and his teacher from his, as a tradition of Moses from Sinai. Mishna *Eduyyot* 8.7 quotes R. Joshua as using the same words as are ascribed to R. Eliezer in Mishna *Yadaim, loc. cit.*, with regard to a tradition under discussion there. "R. Joshua said, 'I have a tradition from Rabban Johanan ben Zakkai, who had it from his teacher, and his teacher from his, as a tradition of Moses from Sinai.'" Unfortunately, in that instance, we have no corresponding text enabling us to determine with certainty whether these were the actual words of

R. Joshua, or an emendation of his comment by the editor of the Mishna. We may perhaps assume that R. Joshua, like R. Eliezer, stated in fact that Rabban Johanan ben Zakkai had this tradition from "the Pairs," and they from the Prophets. This is the more likely as the Mishna itself (*Peah* 2.6) quotes a certain R. Miasha, who was a contemporary of Rabban Gamaliel I, as stating that he had a tradition from "the Pairs," who had received it from the Prophets, as a tradition of Moses from Sinai. It thus appears fairly certain that in the school of Rabban Johanan ben Zakkai it was held that he was the successor to "the Pairs"; and that the authority which had been received by Hillel and Shammai from their predecessors, and by them from the Prophets, had been inherited by the School established by Rabban Johanan ben Zakkai.

13. While the custom of reciting the Chapters of the Fathers every Sabbath afternoon is *recorded* only in Gaonic times (see references given in my little work, *Ha-Perushim ve-Anshe Keneset ha-Gedolah,* p. 24), it doubtless originated much earlier. This can be demonstrated from the fact that on Sabbath afternoons the recital of each chapter is preceded with the statement "All Israel has a share in the Future World etc.", a passage found only in Mishna *Sanhedrin,* Chap. 10 (see my discussion of the text in the work just cited, p. 104), and only in some versions of that text. The natural explanation of this addition to each chapter of the Chapters of the Fathers is that the passage originally introduced the treatise *Abot ;* and was retained in the oral recitation of the treatise, and of each chapter. Because of the consolatory nature of the assertion it was natural to repeat it before each chapter, when the treatise was divided into chapters. But the use of the norm at the beginning of Mishna *Abot* points to a time when the whole treatise was part of Mishna *Sanhedrin,* Chap. 10. The assertion that "All Israel has a share in the future world" was followed with a few paragraphs, now preserved in Mishna *Sanhedrin,* Chap. 10, enumerating the exceptions. (That these paragraphs of Mishna *Sanhedrin* originally followed *Abot* is clear from the final sections of ARN I, which are commentaries on them.) Curiously enough, the recital of each chapter of *Abot* on Sabbath afternoons is followed by what is now a norm toward the end of Mishna *Makkot.* These data lead to the conclusion that in ancient times Mishna *Sanhedrin* ended, as it still does in some versions, with the chapter dealing with the Future World. This chapter began with the statement that "All Israel has a share in the Future World." That statement was followed by the earliest version of *Abot,* probably containing only the statement of the chain of tradition. That was followed by what is now the treatise *Makkot,* which in some texts is still combined with Mishna *Sanhedrin* (see J. N. Epstein, *Mabo le-Sifrut ha-Tannaim,* p. 417), and it ended with the statement of R. Hananiah ben Aqashiah, now found in Mishna *Makkot* 3.16. When the treatise *Abot* was enlarged through the addition of new material (see *Mabo le-Mesiktot Abot,*

135

p. 106), it was separated from Mishna *Sanhedrin,* the opening norm being retained in the final chapter of the Mishna.

In the light of this development it is clear that the custom of reciting on every Sabbath between Passover and Shabuot the original treatise of *Abot,* containing only the chain of tradition, goes back to very early times, before *Abot* was separated from Mishna *Sanhedrin.* The separation was probably made by either R. Akiba, or his disciples, or R. Judah the Patriarch.

14. See *The Pharisees,* third ed. pp. 115 ff. and 641 ff.

15. I use the term *Proto-Pharisaic* for the teachers through whom the Pharisaic traditions were transmitted, in the fifth, fourth, and third centuries B.C.E., to the earliest Pharisaic authorities known by name viz., Simeon the Righteous and Antigonus of Socho, and their disciples, José ben Joezer of Zeredah and José b. Johanan of Jerusalem, the first of the "Pairs." All the Proto-Pharisaic teachers transmitted their teachings anonymously; so that not one name of this series of scholars is known to us, nor was apparently known to generations following them. Yet there can be no doubt of the existence of such teachers. They were the constituent members of the Great Synagogue; and they were the scholars from whom the Pharisaic teachers derived the Oral Law. I have shown in *The Pharisees* (third ed., pp. 107 ff. and 116 ff.) that it is clear that some of these traditions were known to biblical writers; and apparently they were opposed by pre-Pharisaic High Priests, as forcefully as by the Sadducees of later times. I have elsewhere (*Conservative Judaism,* Summer, 1958, pp. 1 ff.; and *Ha-Perushim ve-Anshe Keneset ha-Gedolah,* p. 64) contended that this anonymity was deliberate, arising from the doctrine of these early scholars that name-immortality suggests lack of belief in soul-immortality, and that the hunger for posthumous fame as for fame in life is inconsistent with purity of service to the Deity. This seems to be true of the Second Isaiah, whose name could hardly have been obliterated, except through his own wish. Prof. E. Bickerman has argued that similar anonymity was characteristic of the early scholars of the Greek schools (*Revue d. Études Bilbliques* LIX, 1952, pp. 49 ff.). However, the examples cited from the Prophets and the Psalms, as well as later literature, suggest a deliberate quest for oblivion among the early Jewish scholars.

16. See *Introduction to the Treatises Abot and ARN,* pp. 233 ff.

17. Professor Saul Lieberman suggests to me that the use of the term *qabbalah* for the Prophetic literature and the Hagiographa, *i.e.,* the whole Bible outside the Pentateuch, may be associated with the concept that the Prophets and other sacred writers "received" their tradition orally. Their writings had the status of such tradition. For this use of the term *qabbalah,* see, for example, Mishna *Ta'anit* 2.1.

18. *Sifra Behuqotai, perek* 8, end, 112c.

19. *B. Yebamot* 72b.

20. *B. Gittin, loc. cit.*

21. Presumably R. Johanan based his opinion on the statement of the Mishna *Hagigah* 1.8, which enumerates large sections of the Oral Tradition having no basis whatsoever in Scripture. "[The laws permitting] release of vows [by a scholar] hang in the air and have nothing [in Scripture] to which they can be attached. The laws of the Sabbath, of the festival offerings, of *me'ilot* ["misuse of holy objects for profane purposes"] are like mountains hanging on a hair ; for the verses [in Scripture] are few, but the rules are many. The civil law, the laws of sacrifice, the laws of purity and impurity, and the laws governing sex relations are based on [specific] verses, and are of the essence of Torah." The passage is cited in *Tosefta 'Erubin,* end, (ed. Lieberman, p. 138), as well as in *Tosefta Hagigah,* Chap. 1, end, p. 379. In both passages of *Tosefta,* R. Joshua offers the following comment on this Mishna: "Tongs are made with tongs. How then were the first tongs made? Obviously, it was a [Divine] creation." R. Joshua suggests that while innumerable details of the laws (which are without support in Scripture) were derived from general statements, the original norms on which they are based must have been Divine revelations preserved orally. The statement in the Mishna is cited by R. Joshua, and thus surely antedates him, reflecting the view of Pharisaism before the time of R. Akiba. See the discussion of the meaning of the Mishna in Professor Saul Lieberman's *Tosefta Kifeshutah, 'Erubin,* pp. 468 ff. ; and *Hagigah,* p. 1286 ; as well as the comment of Ch. Albeck in his edition of the Mishna, II, p. 510, and J. N. Epstein, *Mebuot le-Sifrut ha-Tannaim,* pp. 18 ff., 47 ff.

22. *Cf.* I Sam. 9.19 ; I Chron. 9.22 ; *Tosefta Ta'anit* 3(4).2, ed. Lieberman p. 337.

NOTE TO APPENDIX B TO CHAPTER II

1. This is the reading of the Vatican Ms. of this part of *Yerushalmi,* and is accepted by Professor Louis Ginzberg, in his *Commentary on the Yerushalmi* IV, p. 57.

NOTES TO APPENDIX D TO CHAPTER IX

1. It is possible that the statement is to be interpreted to mean that the Sabbath occurred on the ninth of Ab ; and that the Temple was set afire toward evening.

2. If three months had thirty days each, as was possible when the New Moon was fixed by observation rather than by calculation, there would have been 119 days. That would not affect the argument here presented, as shown below.

3. I use the term "Year I" for the first year of the changed system, and Year IV for the fourth year; the Temple was destroyed in the Year IV. The numbers do not indicate the calendar years, which began in Tishri, but the Temple years which began with the first of Nisan.

4. If there were 119 days between Nisan I and Ab 1 the total might be as large as 1,186 days. In that event, there would be 169 weeks and one day. That would not affect the argument, see below.

5. If the total was 1,186 days, the first of Nisan in Year I occurred on Friday.

6. This would be true also if the first of Nisan of Year I was Friday; for then the clan of Jehoiarib would begin its ministry on the following day. That is why the possibility that 119 days elapsed between Nisan I and Ab 1 of Year IV does not affect the argument in the text.

7. The description of the vandalism of the Babylonians during the final days of the Solomonic Temple in *Tosefta Ta'anit* 4(3)10, ed. Zuckermandel p. 220, ed. Lieberman, p. 340, may represent a vivid recollection of what happened when the Temple was sacked by the Romans. In that event, it is possible that the ninth of Ab was on the final Sabbath, instead of the eighth of Ab, as indicated above. If so, the second of Ab was a Sabbath. The first Sabbath of Nisan of Year I might, in that event, have been the second of Nisan, for 168 weeks separated the first Sabbath of Nisan in Year I from the first Sabbath of Ab in Year IV.

BIBLIOGRAPHY

Mishna, ed. Romm, reprinted by *Pardes,* New York, 1953.
Mishna, ed. Ch. Albeck, Jerusalem—Tel Aviv, 1952-58.
Mishna, ed. W. H. Lowe, Cambridge, 1883.
Mishna, Ms. Parma (Facsimile ed.).
Mishna, Ms. Budapest (Facsimile ed.).
Mishna *Tamid,* ed. A. Brody, Uppsala, 1936.
Tosefta, ed. M. S. Zuckermandel, reprinted with new Foreword by Rabbi Saul Lieberman, Jerusalem, 1930.
Tosefta Zeraim, ed. S. Lieberman, New York, 1955.
Tosefta Mo'ed, ed. S. Lieberman, New York, 1962.
Tosefta Yebamot, Ketubot, Nedarim, Nazir, New York, 1967.
Abot of R. Nathan, ed. S. Schechter, reprinted New York, 1945.
Mekilta, ed. H. S. Horovitz—I. A. Rabin, Berlin, 1928.
Mekilta of R. Simeon b. Yohai, ed. J. N. Epstein—E. Z. Melammed, Jerusalem, 1955.
Sifra, ed. I. H. Weiss, Vienna, 1862.
Sifra, with commentary ascribed to Rabbi Samson of Sens, and with notes of Rabbi Jacob David, Warsaw, 1866.
Sifra, with commentary of Rabbi Z. H. Rapaport, *Vayyiqra,* Vilna, 1845 ; *Zav,* Zhitomir, 1866 ; *Shemini-Tazria,* Przemysl, 1901.
Sifra, with commentary of Rabbenu Hillel, ed. Schachne Koleditzy, Jerusalem, 1961.
Sifra, Facsimile ed. of Ms. Assemani (Vatican) 66, New York, 1956.
Sifre Numbers and Deuteronomy, ed. M. Friedmann, Vienna, 1864.
Sifre, with commentary of Rabbi Naphthali Zebi Yehudah Berlin, Jerusalem, Vol. I, 1959 ; Vol. II, 1960 ; Vol. III, 1961.
Sifre Numbers and *Sifra Zutta,* ed. H. S. Horovitz, reprinted Jerusalem, 1966.
Sifre Deuteronomy, ed. H. S. Horovitz—L. Finkelstein, Berlin, 1939.
Midrash Tannaim, ed. D. Z. Hoffman, Berlin, 1908.
Seder 'Olam Rabbah, ed. B. Ratner, Vilna, 1897.
Seder 'Olam Rabbah, ed. Alexander Marx, Berlin, 1903.
Megillat Ta'anit, ed. Hans Lichtenstein, *Hebrew Union College Annual,* VIII-IX (1931-32), pp. 318 ff.
Masseket Soferim, ed. M. Higger, New York, 1937.
Masseket Semahot, ed. M. Higger, New York, 1931.
Yerushalmi, Venice (1523?).
Yerushalmi, Sheqalim, ed. A. Sofer, New York, 1951.
Babli, ed. Romm, reprinted New York, 1919.
Babli, Ta'anit, ed. H. Malter, (large ed. with variants and cros references, as well as commentary), New York, 1930.
Bereshit R., ed. J. Theodor—Ch. Albeck, Berlin 1901-1926.
Vayyiqra Rabba, ed. M. Margoliot, Jerusalem, 1953.
Midrash Rabbah, ed. Romm, Vilna, 1887.
Debarim Rabba, ed. S. Lieberman, Jerusalem, 1939.
Pesiqta d'R. Kahana, ed. B. Mandelbaum, New York, 1962.

Midrash Tanhumah, New York—Berlin, 1927.
Midrash Tanhumah, ed. S. Buber, Vilna, 1913.
Midrash Tehillim, ed. S. Buber, Vilna, 1891.
Midrash Mishle, ed. S. Buber, Vilna, 1893.
Pesiqta Zutreta, ed. S. Buber, Vilna, 1880.
Midrash Hagadol, Bereshit, ed. M. Margoliot, Jerusalem, 1947.
Midrash Hagadol, Shemot, ed. M. Margoliot, Jerusalem, 1956.
Midrash Hagadol, Vayyiqra, ed. E. N. Rabinowitz, New York, 1930.
Midrash Hagadol, Bamidbar, ed. Z. M. Rabinowitz, Jerusalem, 1967.
R. H. Charles, *Apochrypha and Pseudepigrapha of the O.T.,* Oxford, 1913.
S. Schechter, *Documents of Jewish Sectaries,* Cambridge, 1910.
Ch. Rabin, *The Zadokite Documents,* Oxford, 1934.
A. M. Haberman, *Megillot Midbar Yehudah,* Israel, 1959.

Abramson, S., *Querobot le-Hatan, Tarbiz,* XV (1943), pp. 50 ff.
Adeni, Solomon, *Meleket Shelomoh,* published in ed. of Mishna, New York.
Aharoni, Y., in D. Winton Thomas, *Archaeology and Old Testament Study,* (Oxford 1967), pp. 385 ff.
Albeck, Ch., *Das Buch d. Jubilaeen u. d. Halacha,* Berlin, 1930.
Albright, W. F., *From the Stone Age to Christianity,* Baltimore, 1940.
Baron, S., *The Jewish Community,* Philadelphia, 1942.
Bickerman, E., *Benediction et Prière,* in *Révue des Etudes Bibliques,* LIXX (1962), pp. 524 ff.
Cross, F. R., *The Ancient Library of Qumran,* Garden City, N.Y., 1958.
Engel, R. Joseph, *Gilyone ha-Shas, Moed,* Vienna, 1929.
Epstein, J. N., *Mabo le-Nusah ha-Mishnah,* Jerusalem, 1948.
Epstein, J. N.—E. Z. Melammed, *Mebuot le-Sifrut ha-Tannaim,* Jerusalem, 1957.
Finkelstein, L., *Akiba, Scholar, Saint and Martyr,* New York, 1936.
  The Pharisees, third ed., Philadelphia, 1962.
  The Oldest Midrash, published in *Harvard Theological Review,* XXXI (1939), pp. 291 ff.
  Pre-Maccabean Documents in the Passover Haggadah, published in *Harvard Theological Review,* XXXV (1942), pp. 291 ff.; XXXVI (1943), pp. 1 ff.
  The Development of the Amidah, published in *Jewish Quarterly Review,* N.S. XVI (1925-26), pp. 1-43 ; 127-170.
  The Meaning of the Word PORES, published in *Jewish Quarterly Review,* N.S. XXXII (1941-42), pp. 387 ff.
  The Origin of the Synagogue, published in *Proceedings of the American Academy for Jewish Research* (1928-29), pp. 49 ff.

Ha-Perushim ve-Anshe Keneset ha-Gedolah, New York, 1950.

Mabo li-Mesiktot Abot ve-Abot d'R. Natan, New York, 1950.

Fleischer, E., *Piyyute Yannai 'al Mishmerot ha-Kohanim, Sinai* LXIV, 1929, pp. 176 ff.

Fraenkel, Z., *Ueber d. Einfluss d. palaestinischen Exegese auf die alexandrinische Hermeneutik*, Leipzig, 1851.

Ginzberg, L., *Perushim ve-Hiddushim bi-Yerushalmi* (cited as "*Commentary on the Yerushalmi*") Vols. I-III, New York, 1941 ; Vol. IV (ed. D. Weiss), New York, 1961. *Ginze Schechter*, New York, 1928-29.

Jacob, B., *Im Namen Gottes*, Breslau, 1903.

Kahle, P., *Die Masoreten d. Westens*, reprinted, Hildesheim, 1967.

Kauffmann, Yehezkel, *Toledot ha-Emunah ha-Yisrealit*, Vols. I-VIII, Tel Aviv, 1937—Jerusalem, 1956.

Klein, S. *Neue Beitraege z. gesch. u. Geog. Galilaeas*, Vienna, 1923. *Ma'amarim Shonim le-Haqirat Erez Yisrael*, Vienna, 1924, pp. 3 ff.

Lieberman, S., *Greek in Jewish Palestine*, New York, 1942.

Hellenism in Jewish Palestine, New York, 1950.

Yevanim ve-Yavnut be-Erez Yisrael, Jerusalem, 1962.

Tosefet Rishonim, Jerusalem, Vol. I, 1937 ; Vol. II, 1938 ; Vols. III-IV, 1939.

Tosefta Kifeshutah, New York, Vols. I-II, 1956 ; Vols. III, IV, V, 1962 ; Vol. VI, 1967.

Kalos, Killusin in *'Ale Ayyin, Z. Schocken Jubilee Volume*, Jerusalem, 1908-12, pp. 75 ff.

Horaot Nishkahot, in *Leshonenu* XXXII, 1968, pp. 89 ff.

Loew, Leopold, *Gesammelte Schriften*, Szegedin, 1889-1900.

Meir Simhah, R., of Dvinsk, *Meshech Hokmah*, Riga, 1927.

Meyer, Eduard, *Ursprung u. Anfaenge d. Christentums*, Vol. II, Stuttgart, 1921.

Pardo, R. David, *Sifre debe Rab*, Salonica, 1799. *Hasde David*, Livorno, 1776-90.

Rosenfeld, A., *Authorized Kinot for the Ninth of Ab* (Hebrew and English), London, 1965.

Sanders, J. A., *The Psalm Scroll of Cave II*, Oxford, 1965.

E. Schuerer, *Gesch. d. Volkes Israel*, fourth ed., Vols. I-III, Leipzig, 1907.

Talmon, S., in *Mehgarim bi-Megillot ha-Genuzot*, (*Sukenik Memorial Vol.*), Jerusalem, 1961 (pp. 77 ff.).

Zimmermann, H., *Elohim*, Berlin, 1900.

Zulay, M., in *Yediot ha-Makon le-Heqer ha-Shirah ha-Ibrit*, V, Jerusalem, 1939, pp. 109 ff.

INDEX TO PASSAGES CITED

This Index includes references to the Hebrew Scriptures, the New Testament, Apocrypha, Pseudepigrapha, Babylonian and Palestinian Talmuds, Mishna, Tosefta, and other rabbinic works, as well as Josephus.

The numbers on the right refer to pages.

145

INDEX TO SUBJECTS

Jedaiah, clan of, 51, 58, 59, 61, 65, 66, 67, 69, 102, 103, 109; ministry of, 60, 63, 129 n. 8, 130 n. 13, 15.

Jehoiachin, King, 18, 26.

Jehoiakim, King, 17.

Jehoiarib, clan of, 58, 59, 60, 61, 62, 64, 65, 69, 129 n. 9; ministry of, 63, 106 ff., 129 n. 8, 130 n. 13, 15, 16, 138 n. 6.

Jeremiah, 2, 14, 16, 17, 19, 20, 21, 22, 26, 27, 28, 29, 35, 36, 42, 74, 84, 85, 93, 94, 118 n. 2, 119 n. 6.

Jesus, 133 n. 3.

Jeshua, 101, 107.

Job, 27, 28, 29, 88, 120 n. 1.

Joel, 14, 16; authorship of, 17.

Johanan, (R.), 15, 86, 91, 92, 137 n. 21.

Johanan ben Zakkai, 82, 134 n. 12.

Joiakim, 101.

Jonah, 26, 27, 28.

Jose ben Joezer, 80, 136 n. 15.

Jose ben Zeredah, 81, 136 n. 15.

José the Galilean, 120 n. 4, 133 n. 1.

Joseph, Rab, 113 n. 1.

Joshua, 58, 87, 89; authority of, 84; transmitter of Torah, 77, 78, 79, 81, 83, 86.

Joshua, R., 134 n. 12, 137 n. 21.

Joshua ben Hananya, 131 n. 21(b).

Joshua ben Levi, 47, 48.

Josiah, King, 8, 36, 56, 73, 113 n. 1.

Jozadak, 61.

Jubilee Year, 109, 110.

Jubilees, Book of, 8, 133 n. 3; date of, 113 n. 4; midrashic exegesis in, 113 n. 5.

Judah, land of, 70, 71.

Judah ben Ilai, 47, 95, 123, 131 n. 21(a).

Judah the Patriarch, 82, 134 n. 12, 136 n. 13.

Judean Scrolls, 113 n. 2.

Judges, and Torah, 78, 79, 81, 86, 87, 88.

Kings, 70; written by Jeremiah, 21.

Koheleth. See Ecclesiastes.

Lamentations, 21.

Law, Interpretation of, 5, 12.

Levites, 36, 88; divisions of 49, 50; Jerusalemites, function of, 53, 54; ma'amadot, 53 ff., 70, 103 ff.; mishmarot, 51 ff., 57, 70 ff.; provincials, and Temple, 55 ff., 70, 71, 73.

Ma'amadot, 50, 53; defined, 49; date of establishment, 69; end, 75; Israelite, 68, 104 ff.; meanings, 103 ff.; and Shema', 110 ff.; and synagogue, 74, 75. See also Levites; Priests.

Maimonides, 95, 105, 108.

Malachi, 89, 118 n. 2; and Torah, 78, 80, 81, 89.

Malkiah, clan of, 61, 65, 66, 67, 102, 103.

Maloki, 102.

Maluk, 102.

Maluki, 102.

Manasseh, King, 8, 36, 48, 56, 73, 74.

Maoziah, clan of, 63, 129 n. 8, 130 n. 15.

Matthew, 133 n. 3.

Meir, 76.

Meir Simhah of Dvinsk, 95.

Mekilta, 10, 11, 12, 29, 46 ff.

Mekilta of R. Simeon, 31, 32, 120 n. 3.

Men of the Great Synagogue, 19, 42, 44, 48, 118 n. 4; transmitters of Torah, 77, 78, 80, 81, 82, 83, 89, 90,

Meremot, 52.

Miasha, R., 135 n. 12.

Micah, 14.

Midrash, 13, 86.

Midrashic method, 8, 113 n. 5, 115 n. 7C.

Midrash ha-Gadol, 33, 119 n. 6.

Midrash Hakamim, 40, 47, 121 n. 3, 124 n. 6, 125 n. 10, 14, 15, 126 n. 16, 18, 127 n. 28.

Midrash Tannaim, 16 ff., 33 ff., 43 ff., 124 n. 6, 8, 125 n. 10, 12, 14, 126 n. 15.

Mishmarot, 50-54, 57, 58, 68, 74; date of establishment, 69, 70, 128 n. 2; defined, 49, 50-52; and Shema', 110-11; system during Second Commonwealth, 72 ff. See also Levites; Priests.

Mishna, 6, 11, 12.

M. Abot, 8, 32, 77 ff., 83; recitation of, 135 n. 13.

M. Ta'anit, 8, 49 ff.

Modim, part of 'amidah, 38; meaning of, 126 n. 18.

Mordecai, prayer of, 42.

Morning-Bathers, 9, 10, 116 n. 16.

Simeon the Righteous, 121 n. 4, 136 n. 15; transmitter of Torah, 77, 78, 81, 85.
Solomon, King, 52, 58, 70, 71, 99, 119 n. 4; and prayer, 38, 41, 42.
Solomon of Adeni, 97, 128 n. 5.
Song of David, 19, 21, 22.
Song of Songs, 118 n. 4.
Study, merit of, 121 n. 4; as worship, 68.
Sukkot, 65, 93, 107, 129 n. 8, 131 n. 21(b).
Synagogue, 9, 47-8, 121 n. 1, 122 n. 2; and ma'amadot, 74-5.
Tarfon, 121 n. 4.
Temple, 51, 63, 68, 88, 94 ff.; Court of, 115 n. 7B; defilement of, 36, 48, 123; donations to, 54.

Temple of Arad, 53.
Tephillin, 74, 105-6.
Tetragrammaton, 116 n. 9, 11, 13, 126 n. 21; use of, 8-10.
Titus, 78.
Torah, 84, 91-2, 121 n. 4, 132 n. 1; preservation, 24; reading of, 68, 74; transmission, 30, 77 ff.; study of, 31.
Tosefta, 6, 12.
Well of the Golah, 95.
Yabneh, 82.
Zadok, 58.
Zechariah, 34, 89, 117 n. 2, 118 n. 2; transmitter of Torah, 78, 80, 81.
Zedekiah, King, 17, 36.
Zerubabel, 60 ff.; 71, 101.